The Challenge of Toddlers

Also by Jeanne Warren Lindsay

(Partial listing)

Your Baby's First Year

Teen Dads: Rights, Responsibilities and Joys

School-Age Parents: Challenge of Three-Generation Living

Teenage Couples — Expectations and Reality

Teenage Couples — Caring, Commitment and Change

Teenage Couples — Coping with Reality

Pregnant? Adoption Is an Option

Parents, Pregnant Teens and the Adoption Option

Do I Have a Daddy? A Story for a Single-Parent Child

By Jeanne Lindsay and Jean Brunelli

Your Pregnancy and Newborn Journey

*Nurturing Your Newborn: Young Parents' Guide
to Baby's First Month*

By Jeanne Lindsay and Sally McCullough

Discipline from Birth to Three

By Jeanne Lindsay and Sharon Enright

*Books, Babies and School-Age Parents:
How to Teach Pregnant and Parenting Teens to Succeed*

The Challenge of Toddlers

— For Teen Parents —

Parenting Your Child from One to Three

Jeanne Warren Lindsay, MA, CFCS

Morning Glory Press

Buena Park, California

The Challenge of Toddlers
is part of the six-book *Teens Parenting* series. Other titles are:
Your Pregnancy and Newborn Journey: A Guide for Pregnant Teens
Nurturing Your Newborn: Young Parents' Guide
to Baby's First Month
Your Baby's First Year: A Guide for Teen Parents
Discipline from Birth to Three: How Teen Parents Can Prevent
and Deal with Discipline Problems with Babies and Toddlers
Teen Dads: Rights, Responsibilities and Joys

Library of Congress Cataloging-in-Publication Data
Lindsay, Jeanne Warren.
    The Challenge of Toddlers : for teen parents : parenting your
child from one to three / Jeanne Warren Lindsay. -- Rev. ed.
        p.   cm. -- (Teens parenting)
    Includes bibliographical references and index.
    Summary: Describes for teenage parents the development and
special needs of children from one to three and offers advice and
comments from many young parents themselves.
    ISBN 1-932538-07-0. -- ISBN 1-932538-06-2 (Paper)
    1. Toddlers--United States--Juvenile literature. 2. Child rearing
--United Sates--Juvenile literature. 3. Teenage parents--United
States--Juvenile literature. [1. Teenage parents. 2. Parenting. 3.
Child development.] I. Title. II. Series: Lindsay, Jeanne Warren.
Teens parenting.
HQ774.5.L56 1998
649'. 122--dc21   98-35683
                                                                      CIP
                                                                        AC

MORNING GLORY PRESS, INC.
6595 San Haroldo Way   Buena Park, CA 90620-3748
714/828-1998   1-888/612-8254
Printed and bound in the United States of America

Contents

Preface

If you've been a parent for at least a year, or if you will be the parent of a child aged one to three, this book is for you. It's especially for you if you're a teenage parent.

Teenage mothers and fathers share their parenting insights throughout these pages. They speak from their realities, the realities of teenagers who are also parents. They share their dreams and their frustrations, their hopes and fears for their children and themselves.

Child-rearing is not the only topic discussed in these chapters. Tips for meeting your own needs are also offered. One of the most important things you can do for your child is to make a satisfying life for yourself as well as for him/her. You'll be able to parent better if your own life is going well. Caring for an active toddler may make it harder for you to follow your dreams. That's why it's even more important for you to make a plan now to start working toward those goals and those dreams.

During your baby's first year, you were probably absorbed in childcare. Caring for baby was an all-consuming task. Your personal needs may have received little attention. By the time your baby is a year old, however, you may realize you need to get on with your own life, even as you continue caring for your child.

This book provides a guide for caring for children aged one to three years. It covers such topics as child development, nutrition, sleep, language development, health and safety, and activities for toddlers. Throughout, comments from young parents reinforce the concepts presented.

Other chapters focus on the needs of teen parents themselves. While the entire book is directed to both mothers and fathers, two chapters discuss two-parent issues specifically. "Dad's Ahead If He's Involved" advocates for strong two-parent cooperation in child-rearing when feasible, whether or not the parents are living together.

Teenage parents may be married to each other, they may be living together, be "together" but living apart, or one or both may be with a different partner. "The Partnership Challenge" provides a discussion of these various relationships. Young parents share insights gained from their experience with partners.

One chapter focuses on the impact on parenting of parents' gang involvement. Another is for young mothers who have had to cope with sexual and other abuse as they grew up, and on protecting one's child from abuse.

The final chapter provides suggestions for you as you plan your future life. The importance of continuing your education, obtaining job skills, and becoming independent is emphasized.

Parenting a toddler is a difficult task for parents of any age. Combine this task with the special needs of adolescents, and it becomes a gigantic challenge. I hope this book will help you in your quest for a satisfying life for yourself even as you parent your toddler.

Jeanne Warren Lindsay   January, 2004

Foreword

I wish there had been a Jeanne Lindsay in my life in the late 1940s when I was having babies. Although I was a college graduate, married to a loving, supportive husband, I felt parenthood was the most important job I had ever undertaken, yet the one for which I was least prepared. I could have used the practical insights that Lindsay passes on to young parents that are reassuring, challenging, and fun.

Ideally, parenting should be enjoyed, as well as understood. This is not easy if the pregnancy was unplanned or unwanted. But the bond that a young woman usually begins to develop with the fetus becomes full-blown when a new human being emerges from her labor.

Most of us can deal with the infant stage, because we love to feel needed. A cuddly infant is dependent, and gradually grows responsive to our display of affection — most rewarding! But when that infant turns into an active toddler with the curiosity of an explorer, the imagination of an artist, and the rebelliousness of an adolescent, watch out.

This is when the understanding, tact, challenge, patience, and yes, endurance, of mothers and fathers is summoned.

If we parents cultivate these characteristics, then we find the *joy* of watching a unique personality unfold before our eyes. With eyes to see and ears to hear, we are privileged to be part of the world of very interesting little people. This is apparent in Lindsay's book. Whether she is dealing with motor skills, feeding, bedtime, safety, active play, or planning for the future, there is the fun of the present developmental stage as well as the hope of the good life to come.

When I was director of the Margaret Hudson Program for teenage parents in Tulsa, Oklahoma, I found the fun of the hundreds of babies with whom we dealt was their differences. Surely there were common aspects of development, but also, very early, they had distinct personalities.

These babies enriched the parents, the staff, and each other as they learned to respond to their environment. We had the sense of being potters, experimenting with lumps of human clay. I, for one, would find myself praying to my God, "Oh, Lord, make me a worthy potter of this precious little vessel."

The teen mothers and fathers quoted in this book are confronting the realities of parenthood. One would hope that they, and those who come after, would find the supports in our society that provide the needed guidance and encouragement to produce competent, healthy children. *The Challenge of Toddlers* is one of these supports.

(The Reverend) Lois H. Gatchell
Deacon, Episcopal Diocese of Oklahoma

Acknowledgments

I am grateful to Sally and Stewart McCullough, Diane Smallwood, Jean Brunelli, Jan Stanton, Pat Alviso, and Pati Lindsay who made time to read and critique *The Challenge of Toddlers*, and to those who read the first edition. Their comments were invaluable.

Perhaps even more important is the input from teen parents, the young people we interviewed, and whose wisdom is scattered throughout the book. About 130 teen parents were interviewed for this book and the others in the *Teens Parenting* **Series**, and many of them are quoted here. Those most recently interviewed and quoted include Yadira Hernandez, Grace Kong, Genavieve Macias, Alexis Hernandez, and Elizabeth Jimenez.

Others quoted and included in earlier editions as well as this one include Alysson Hall, Tim Whitehead, Andrea Gonzales, Carlos Smith, Antonee Williams, Brandi Hatch, Erika Madrid, Ernie Mejia, Gabriel Garcia, Priscilla Correa, Harmony Tortorice, Isabel Franco, Jessica Marquez, Juan Zepeda, Katie Stonebarger, Katrina Amaya, Laura Lilio, Laura Moran,

Maria Almarez Valtierrez, Melisa Romero, Mira Montepio, Noel Mejia, Racheal Malonay, Robin Gardner, Robin Stanley, Rosa Paez, Shamika Mills, Stephanie Whittaker, Stormi Lopez, Tiffany Torres, Carlos Garcia, Tina Mondragon, Veronica Bosquez, Yvette Aguirre, and Yolanda Torres.

Also Lissa Mosqueda, Albert Aguilar, Angela and Chris Carena, Jessica Aguilar, Lorena Martinez Silva, Linda Solano, Karen Perlas Gagui, Jennifer Launchbury, Michelle Conway, Cynthia and Roman Mendoza, Rebecca Reeves, Deanne Andringa Grachen, Karen Smith Lind, Terri Emerson, Alicia Ochoa, Julie Farah, Lupe Cordi, Michelle Bragdon, Angelica Ramos, Tammy Peace, Judy Chavez, Dolores Cruz Corrales, Ardell Hucko, Cynthia Mendoza, Lynetta Allen, Jo Ann Harris, Anita Smith, Michelle Johnson, Gabriel and Tammy Ayala, and Larry Jaurequi. Others are quoted and acknowledged in the other books in the *Teens Parenting* **Series.**

The late David Crawford, teacher in the Teen Parent Program, William Daylor High School, Sacramento, supplied most of the photographs retained from earlier editions. Carole Blum photographed students in the Teen Parent Program, Tracy High School, Cerritos, CA, especially for this edition. A few other photos were contributed by Cheryl Boeller and Bob Lindsay.

Tim Rinker is the cover artist, and Steve Lindsay helped design the book. I am grateful for the contributions of all of these talented people.

Nora Simoés helped with the proof-reading and kept Morning Glory Press alive and well during book production time. I thank her for her valuable support.

Thank you, Bob, for being supportive and caring no matter what else is going on in our lives. I love you very.

Jeanne Warren Lindsay
Buena Park, California

To the young parents who shared so freely
and taught me so much
as we worked together.

Your child is an exciting challenge.

1

He's One —
Soon He'll Be Running

- **Tremendous Changes in Both of You**
- **Walking Adds Excitement**
- **He Jabbers Before He Talks**
- **She Copies Mom and Dad**
- **Another Baby Already?**
- **From Bottle or Breast to Cup**
- **Your Problem-Solving Toddler**

Brandt walks everywhere. He doesn't want to crawl any more. He walks all around the house, has been for three weeks. He climbs on everything, the chairs, up on the bed. He pushes the chair to the sink and gets up there and plays with the water.

He throws his toys around and makes noises. He pushes the little cars. He doesn't sit still, not even when he's eating. He has to stand up and turn around.

Sheleen, 15 - Brandt, 1

Heidi loves to go to the park. She notices little bugs on the ground, little ants. She'll put her face down close to them, make her little noises, and show me.

She has a little bug catcher toy. When I put a bug in it, she picks it up and looks at it. Then I let the bug go.

I take her for a walk each evening. I teach her things on the way.

We stop every day and look at two dogs and some parakeets behind a fence down the street. One day the owner showed us his birds. She was thrilled.

Jenny, 18 - Heidi, 13 months

Tremendous Changes in Both of You

Now Alice climbs off beds and is learning how to climb up on the bed. I bought her a little skate toy when she was one year old. Within a month, she learned how to get on and off it. She also tried to stop it from going anywhere by climbing on top of it.

She takes off her socks and shoes. She'll put her shirt on. She likes to play peek-a-boo with it. If I'm putting a shirt on, she'll pick up anything around, maybe a nightgown, and put her head through the hole. Then she laughs.

Melanie, 15 - Alice, 13 months

At your child's first birthday you may be startled at the changes you observe in each of you. Your child has developed from a helpless newborn to a whirlwind little person who scoots everywhere and either is walking or will be soon. Even more wonderful than his physical development are the tremendous jumps in his knowledge. He's learning many new things each day, and will continue to progress rapidly with living, learning, and loving under your guidance.

She is learning to walk, which gives her a lovely feeling

of independence. She can ride simple wheel toys. She's discovered that by climbing she can find even more places to explore. She can easily get herself into serious trouble if no one is watching.

Chandler climbs up on the rocking chair and onto the end table. He'll go up on the couch and crawl all the way up to the window.

He will climb up a chair with rungs until it falls over on him, but he's fine when I take the chair off him.

He sits on my little sister's skateboard, and he knows how to make it go.

Recently he started hitting. I tell him that hurts, and I stop him.

Gretchen, 17 - Chandler, 13 months

Your one-year-old has become more interested in toys like shape boxes, formboards, blocks and balls. He especially enjoys these things if someone is nearby to watch or play with him. He enjoys crayons or paints when he is allowed to use them.

She is beginning to talk. She is learning to tell you what she wants through words and gestures. She can follow simple directions. But any understanding of right and wrong, the ability to make simple judgments about behavior, will not even begin to emerge until she is close to two. Even then she often won't know or understand what she should or shouldn't do.

You, too, have probably changed a great deal during your child's first year. Do you feel only a couple of years older than you were BP (Before Pregnancy)? Or are you convinced that you've grown up — matured — at a far faster pace than your birthdays indicate? If you think you're more mature than your actual years, you're probably

right. The responsibilities of parenting for both mothers and
fathers are awesome.

> *The hardest part for me was the change when
> Cassandra was born. I couldn't be myself anymore.
> I couldn't stay young and irresponsible. It was hard
> when we moved out when she was 14 months old. My
> mother was always there doing stuff for me, and
> Cassandra was in the infant center while I was
> in school.*
>
> *I didn't really have a chance to see what it was like
> on my own until we moved. Her father helps me out,
> but taking care of Cassie is still my responsibility. It's
> also amazing how my love for her has grown since
> I've been raising her on my own.*
>
> Kris, 17 - Cassandra, 25 months

Perhaps the biggest change you'll experience with your
child during these toddler years is her individuality and
independence. When she was an infant, it was generally
your job to decide what was best for her. Now she will
insist more and more on making her own decisions.

Walking Adds Excitement

> *If Laramie is holding on to something, he'll walk a
> short distance. He knows how, but he's still kind of
> scared.*
>
> Lynnsey, 19 - Laramie, 1; Kalani, 2

Once your baby starts walking, he's considered a toddler. Being able to walk adds a lot of excitement to his life.
He can explore even more than he could by crawling, no
matter how rapidly he was traveling through your home. He
can move faster, reach higher, and enjoy life even more.

> *Heidi has been walking since she was 10 months
> old, and she started taking steps at 8 months. You tell*

her to come here, and she'll turn around and go the
other way. She's very good at ignoring you. If she's
entering the negative stage, she's getting good at it!

Jenny

Starting to walk at ten months is unusual. Most children
wait until they're 12 to 14 months old, and some are even
older when they take those first steps. If you're nervous
because your 17-month-old son isn't walking yet, talk with
your doctor.

In fact, one of my sons wasn't walking at 17 months so I
took him to the doctor for a checkup. Eric was standing,
hanging on to me when the doctor said, "So, Eric, you

Walking means he can explore even more. Exciting!

aren't walking yet?"

To my amazement, Eric *walked* the few steps over to the doctor! Eric had three older siblings who carried him around, and apparently he hadn't felt the need to walk until that moment.

As preparation for walking, your child will probably cruise from one piece of furniture to another, perhaps for several weeks, before he starts walking on his own. When he finally walks, his balance and coordination won't be well-developed. He'll stretch his arms out to his sides and walk with his legs somewhat spread apart. At first he'll lean slightly forward and take short steps.

Soon his rhythm will improve. Sometime during this stage he'll be able to stoop down, pick something up, and carry it around. Notice how proud he is of this new talent.

Before long he will walk pulling or pushing a toy. This is the time for the corn popper or other push/pull toy. He much prefers a toy that makes a noise as he pulls or pushes it along.

He doesn't need shoes until he starts walking outside. In fact, walking barefoot helps strengthen his feet and arches.

If your floors are a little slick, don't let him try to walk with only socks on his feet. You don't want him to fall — not only because he might hurt himself, but also because falling a lot could discourage him from trying to walk. Walking with bare feet is safer. Slipper socks with non-slip soles are okay.

When you buy shoes for him, be sure they fit well, look comfortable, and aren't too big. There should be about one-half inch of space between his big toe and the end of his shoe. You'll have to replace his shoes often because his feet will grow so quickly. As long as they fit well, it's all right to buy the cheapest brand of shoes you can find. Sneakers are fine.

The mother of twins may have even more of a challenge
when they start crawling, then walking, and then running:

*When they started crawling I went crazy because I
wasn't used to them going around everywhere. I'd be
looking for one, and the other one would run away.
She'd get lost under the tables.*

*Then they started walking, and it was worse! First
they were standing up, hanging on to everything,
trying to reach everything. When they started walking,
then running, it was all over the house. When we go to
stores, they're running all over the place. I'd like to
get two leashes.*

Edie, 17 - Dora and Laura, 26 months

Some parents don't like using a leash on their child.
They say leashes are for puppies. But a leash can be more
comfortable for a child than hanging on to Mom's hand.
Try holding your arm up high as a child must do when he
takes your hand. It's not particularly comfortable. Yet you
know you can't let him run freely in stores, parking lots,
crossing the street, etc. Actually a leash gives him *more*
freedom than does hanging on to your hand.

He Jabbers Before He Talks

*Marty sits there jabbering. He sounds like he
knows what he's talking about, but I can't understand
what he's saying.*

Yumiko, 16 - Marty, 21 months

Talking means jabbering at this stage. He may say his
first word about the time of his first birthday. He will
communicate mostly through gestures for a while yet. He's
eager to learn more words, so play the labeling game with
him. Point to an object and name it, then wait for him to
repeat the name. "Table." "Chair." "Kitty." He may try to

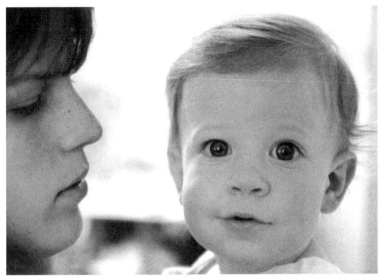

She's learning to talk, but first she jabbers.

say the word after you.

If his word sounds different than yours, don't correct him. Correcting a toddler's speech won't help him. Doing so will either discourage him or bore him. As he begins putting words together, his grammar will likely be different, too. Again, don't correct him. Model proper speech, and he will eventually learn from you. But he won't speak "right" simply because you tell him to do so.

Will your child be bilingual? If two languages are spoken in your home, you probably will want him to learn both. Some people suggest that one parent or caregiver always speak one language to the child, and the other parent or caregiver speak the second language. They feel the child will be able to keep the two languages separate more easily when this happens.

My mom talks to Kamie in Spanish a lot. I've been lagging in that, but I do want her to be bilingual.

Lucas, 21 - Kamie, 21 months

Usually I speak to Vincent in Spanish because I know he'll learn English anyway. In the Infant Center they speak English, but my whole family speaks to him in Spanish.

Vincent wasn't talking that much when he was 2. I put him in a special program at the Infant Center, and he's doing real good now. He's talking a lot more — both English and Spanish.

Mariaeliza, 17 - Vincent, 3

If he's learning two languages, his overall language ability may develop a little more slowly than will the language of a child learning only one. By the time he enters kindergarten, he should speak both languages well. If you can teach your child to become bilingual, you're giving him a valuable gift.

She Copies Mom and Dad

Luciann puts my key in the door and tries to open it.

She takes my car key, and she knows how to open and lock the car, too.

Liliana, 17 - Luciann, 22 months

She likes to copy you. She may feed you pieces of her food, then smile broadly if you take it. She probably loves having you copy her. You can copy her movements and her play activities. She's likely to be delighted.

Copying you is one of her best learning techniques. If you stack a block on top of another, she may do the same thing. If you demonstrate drinking from a cup, she may learn a little more quickly. Her speech, of course, depends a great deal on your modeling.

Your toddler may enjoy showing off. Her sense of humor may be developing nicely:

*Alice makes faces at me, sniffles her nose, laughs.
If she does something people like and they laugh, she
grins real big. Lots of times when she does something
we like, we clap. Then she starts clapping for herself.*
                                                    Melanie

Letting her know you like what she's doing is the best
way to help her develop a good sense of self-esteem. This
won't be hard for you to do because you'll be excited about
her achievements.

*I praise her to make her feel good. You have to
make her feel good so she'll be a good kid.*
    *I wasn't brought up like this. I had a pretty rough
childhood. My mom was young, and she wasn't
around. She left me with my grandparents, and my
grandpa would say, "Oh, you're so stupid."*
                                    Miguel, 20 - Genny, 18 months

Of course you'll *never* talk to your child like Miguel's
grandfather talked to him. You'll also do all you can to
keep other people from putting her down.
    She may be wary of strangers, and even of some people
she knows. She doesn't like to be picked up too quickly by
people she doesn't know well. She's her own person and
doesn't want to be grabbed by adults.

*Alice is real open with most people unless they
want to pick her up right away. When she gets used to
them, she'll go to them.*
                                                    Melanie

Another Baby Already?

Some teen moms have a second baby soon after their
child's first birthday. Life can be difficult for both mom
and toddler.

She's trying hard to figure it out.

When Laramie was born, Kalani wanted a bottle even though she had quit a month earlier. She was real jealous. She'd try to help me, and she wanted to carry him. Of course she might drop him, so I would have to be right behind her.

She'd start to stroke his face, but instead she would hit him. She was just a baby herself.

Lynnsey

Lynnsey lives with her mother and sister. When they're home, she has some help. However, they're usually gone during the day. She commented:

When neither my mom nor my sister is here, and nobody can help me with the kids, it's hard. Sometimes I'm pretty exhausted. To take a shower, for example, I have to wait until they're both sleeping, or until my mom or sister can watch them.

A toddler's emotions come through clearly. If there's already a new baby, she probably will be jealous as well as affectionate toward the new sibling:

When Sylvia was first born, Crystal didn't like her too well and would hit her. I let her help with the baby, and didn't make her feel she was being thrown out. I explained that Sylvia was her baby, too.
Now if anybody makes Sylvia cry, Crystal will protect her. When her little cousin hits Sylvia, Crystal hits him.

Carrie, 18 - Crystal, 31 months; Sylvia, 14 months

If you have two babies under 18 months, you know how hard it is. Hopefully, you have some help at least part of the time.

From Bottle or Breast to Cup

If you haven't started encouraging your child to drink milk, juice, and water from a cup, it's time to do so. Children generally can begin to learn to drink from a cup when they're about nine months old, sometimes even earlier.

Weaning your child from his bottle or your breast is likely to go more smoothly if he's had plenty of time to learn to drink from a cup. Drinking from a cup is quite different from sucking fluid from a bottle.

The milk enters his mouth faster from a cup, and it comes into the front of his mouth instead of the back. Not only will he not be able to suck, he will need to learn how to hold his lower lip along the edge of the cup. Otherwise, the milk will dribble down his chin.

Many children like to use a cup with a drinking spout. They can still suck a little, and the spout is more like a nipple than is the edge of a cup. Transferring to a cup later won't be especially difficult. Also, you'll have far less spilled liquid to clean up if she uses the spouted cup now.

For some children, giving up the bottle is difficult. Some people believe it's easier for the child (and mom and dad) if he switches from his bottle to a cup soon after he's a year old. They feel if he takes his bottle until he's two, for example, he won't want to change — almost like an addiction.

On the other hand, some children appear to need more sucking than others. They suck a thumb or a pacifier for satisfaction. Your child's need to suck will be less as she nears her second birthday. You're the best judge of your child's readiness to give up her bottle.

I always held him when he was little while he took his bottle. I would think that if I was little, and I saw this big bottle in my mouth, nobody around, nobody paying any attention to me, I know how I would feel. So I would always hold him and talk to him while he had his bottle.

Charity, 17 - Casey, 18 months

As you give your baby a bottle of milk, hold her in your lap while you feed her. A child under two will let you know when she's ready to give up the bottle. She will drink a little, then look away or start to play. Two things need to happen at that time:

She has to get enough milk — or get enough calcium from another source such as yogurt and cottage cheese.

You have to be comfortable that she's telling you she

doesn't need the sucking experience any longer.

If your child is hungry at bedtime, give her a light snack or a bottle *before* she goes to bed. Then brush her teeth. If she still needs something to suck on as she drifts off to sleep, give her a bottle of water or a pacifier. Either will satisfy her urge to suck.

There is nothing wrong with going to bed with a bottle of water. That's just fine. It's a nice comforting thing, and all of us like to be comfortable when we go to bed. But it is not good, whatever your child's age, to have milk in that bottle.

If your child goes to sleep with a bottle of milk in his mouth, the sugar in the milk is likely to cause cavities in his teeth — the Nursing Bottle Syndrome. If your toddler wants a bottle at bedtime, put water in the bottle.

Alice will take two or three naps during the day. She's attached to her bottle. At night she has to go to sleep with the bottle, but she doesn't care what's in it. I give her water at night.

If I give her milk in a cup and water in the bottle, maybe she'll quit demanding the bottle so much.

Melanie

Your Problem-Solving Toddler

Todd is so busy. I wonder how he got all that energy. I'll put little crackers in a container, and give him a second container with it. He'll put the crackers back and forth from one to the other. You can see how his little mind works — he'll try to put half on this side and half on the other.

It's unbelievable how much he knows, I guess more than I really give him credit for.

Jill, 18 - Todd, 16 months

As Jill said, you can almost see his mind developing. He's learning more rapidly now than he ever will again. His world is expanding constantly, and he's trying to keep up with it.

For example, Tatiana is using the trial and error method to get on the furniture:

> *We have very tall furniture, tall couches and tall chairs. Tatiana tries to crawl up on them. If she can't, she will go get her own little chair, and use it to stand on to get up on the couch. She likes to sit on the big furniture like we do.*
>
> *Yesterday she was using her little chair to get on the cabinet, but I told her not to. I think that's a little too dangerous.*
>
> Mihaela, 16 - Tatiana, 18 months

Learning through trial and error is a great technique for expanding one's knowledge. You might like to research your child's ability to solve a problem through trial and error. Perhaps she's trying to ride her kiddy car between two pieces of furniture. She discovers she can't get through, so scoots around the furniture instead. That's the trial and error method. Something didn't work, so she tried something else.

If you observe her closely, you'll probably find many examples of her using the trial and error method. It's a wonderful part of her learning.

As you already know, your love and your guidance provide the foundation for your child's future. *You have an exciting challenge.*

She's proud of her new skills.

2

She's Struggling for Independence

- **Toddlers, Like Teenagers, Struggle for Independence**
- **When Your Child Asks for Help**
- **"Terrible Twos"**
- **Her Skills Increase Rapidly**
- **Coping with Fears**
- **Don't Rush Toilet Teaching**
- **Major Tasks for Parents**
- **Most Important Stage in Life**

Jenae is into everything. Today she tried to jump out of her crib.

She loves to sing. Her daddy is in a band and she likes to play the drums. When I ask, "Which CD do you want?" she says, "Dance, dance," and I put one on for her.

She runs around everywhere, learning new things, like a lot of English and Spanish. She puts on her shoes by herself.

Clancy Jane, 17 - Jenae, 23 months

Kamie says "NO." That was one of her first words. She's very talkative.

She puts on her pants and her socks herself. She knows how to open doors, turn on the TV, change the channel.

She's always alert, wanting to do new things, I think maybe because we give her so much attention. When she does things, we clap.

Sometimes I think, what would she be like if I weren't here?

Lucas, 21 - Kamie, 21 months

The runabout stage in a child's life is one of the most difficult for his parents — and for himself. He's trying to move away from being a dependent baby. So far, he has relied on other people for almost everything. Now he wants to be an independent person who makes many of his own decisions and who is rather self-reliant. To develop properly, he needs to take this step, hard as it is on those around him.

Infants are okay, but with toddlers, you have to kind of know what you're doing. And you have to take it one day at a time.

Roseanna, 14 - Felipe, 2

Toddlers, Like Teenagers, Struggle for Independence

The toddler's "negative stage" has been compared to the beginning of puberty. At that time, as you may remember, young people struggle toward becoming adults who make their own decisions. No longer does the adolescent want her parents to "run her life." A great deal of friction occurs in many families at this time because of the parents' desire to stay in control of their teenager's life while the teenager insists on taking over that control. It's often a difficult time for everyone.

Your toddler probably has similar feelings. No, she doesn't want the family car tonight, but she does want to feel she's in control of what she eats, the clothes she wears, when/whether she uses the bathroom, and how long she plays outside. Giving her the opportunity to make some of these decisions may make it easier for her to comply with your wishes when you can't let her choose.

> *Henry is a handful. He doesn't really mess things up and break things, but he climbs, gets into every- thing. I'm constantly having to watch him while I'm doing everything else. It gets very hectic.*
>
> *Every time I tell him to do something, he says "No." Sometimes I put him in the bedroom and shut the door. He'll bang on the door and cry, and that gets on my nerves. When I get really uptight, I let Marvin take care of him, and I get out of the house.*
>
> Olivia, 21 - Henry, 23 months

Teenagers and their parents are ahead if they can each give a little. Perhaps she can't have the family car when- ever she wants it, but she can use it for errands and an occasional evening out with friends. Perhaps she can't stay out as late as she chooses, but maybe she and her parents can arrive at a reasonable compromise.

The consequences of treating adolescents either too strictly or too loosely may be severe. They still need paren- tal support, but they also need to be able to take responsi- bility for their own actions. Teenagers who either lose control of themselves or have never learned to take control of their lives can end up with serious difficulties. They not only may have trouble with other people, but with the law as well.

Parents and toddlers, too, need to adjust to each others' wishes. Your toddler needs to feel she has some control over her life just as you do. A major difference between a teen's struggle for independence and a toddler's struggle is that your toddler can't yet express herself well using words. How would you feel if you had faced the difficulties of adolescence without being able to talk very well? You'd probably feel terribly frustrated.

Compromise and respect are magic ingredients for minimizing the frustrations of living with a toddler. Being sensitive to your child's need to control some aspects of her life will help you understand her behavior better.

When Your Child Asks for Help

As your child becomes more and more independent, she will get upset if she can't do what she wants to do. Yet, her language has not developed enough to tell you what she's feeling and what she wants. She's frustrated, and she can't explain what's wrong because she doesn't know the words. The result may be a tantrum.

Responding when your child asks for help is the best way to cut down on the number of tantrums she will have:

- When your child wants you, stop to see what she wants.
- Provide the help she needs if possible.
- Talk briefly at your child's level of understanding about the event.
- Once you have assisted or comforted and talked to your child, your next step is to leave her alone.

Because of your sensitivity to her needs, your child learns a lot from an interchange like this:

- She learns to use another person (you) as a resource when she can't handle a situation herself.
- She learns that someone thinks her discomfort, excitement, or problem is important, which means she is important.
- Her language skills also get a boost each time this happens.

For more suggestions on helping your child deal with a temper tantrum, see *Discipline from Birth to Three* by Lindsay and McCullough.

"Terrible Twos"

This is Kaylie's "NO" stage. I figure she's at the age where she'll say "No" regardless of what I tell her. Right now, she's mostly running around, screaming and yelling, having fun.

Samantha, 16 - Kaylie, 20 months

Often, people speak of the "Terrible Twos" as if extreme negative behavior suddenly turns up after a child's second birthday. For some children, however, this negative attitude starts as early as 13 or 14 months.

At least by the time he is 17 months old, your child will probably enter this difficult phase. He will often want his own way, no matter what. No longer can you distract him by offering a substitute for the forbidden activity. If he sees that you disapprove of whatever he's doing, he may be even more determined to continue doing it. He will often be hard to live with.

Two thoughts may comfort you. First, this happens to just about every child. His negative actions certainly do not mean you are a poor parent or a terrible person, nor does it mean your child is a brat. Second, his extreme negative behavior will probably go away, or at least become much less intense, within a few months. Perhaps by his second birthday, you will find living with him is a little easier.

For many of us, becoming independent is a real struggle from birth to adulthood. When your toddler seems extra difficult, remember that being a toddler is even harder than caring for one. Your toddler needs all the help and respect you can provide.

If Marty doesn't know how to put something to-
gether, he'll get help. If he wants to read a book, he
brings it to me. He pulls the legs off his plastic doll
and brings them to me. He's pretty independent.
Sometimes if I walk up and try to help him, he seems
to be saying, "Mom, I can do it, leave me alone."

Yumiko, 16 - Marty, 21 months

You still need to be firm about things that matter, but
give him choices whenever possible. Don't say, "Come to
lunch right this minute." Instead, a few minutes before
lunch is ready, ask, "Do you want to wash your hands for
lunch, or shall I help you?" At bedtime you might say,
"Which book do you want me to read tonight?" During this
negative stage, don't ever say, "Do you want lunch?" or
"Do you want to go to bed?" unless you can handle "No"
for your answer.

Avoid showing your power when possible. Don't order
him to do something unless it's really necessary. If it is
necessary, then of course you insist that he go along with
your wishes.

Routines and a regular schedule, not only for bedtime,
but also for meals, naps, baths, and dressing, may help. Let
him do it himself as much as possible. At times, he will
insist on doing it himself when you know he can't possibly
succeed. He may get terribly frustrated, but still won't let
you help him. You need far more tact in dealing with a
toddler than with the most temperamental spouse or em-
ployer in existence. Remember — being tactful is simply
being sensitive to another person's feelings.

How much should you help your child? He needs to
continue to be able to call on you as his resource for help
when he needs it. Sometimes a child of this age seems not
to want to work things out for himself. If he always wants
mother to help him put the puzzle together, either it's too

hard for him, or he isn't learning to be as independent as he should be.

Use your best judgment. Help him when you think he needs you — if he wants you to or will let you. Guide him toward more independence when you think this is advisable.

Her Skills Increase Rapidly

By your child's second birthday, she may be able to pedal a small tricycle. If she has had practice, she can walk down stairs alone, but she still needs to hang on to the stair railing.

Your almost-two-year-old may be running more than she walks. She can walk on low walls if you hold one of her hands. She can even walk a few steps on tiptoe if you show her how.

By this age, she can take off her clothes, and even put most of them back on. It helps if you choose easy-to-put-on clothing. In fact, when you're shopping for her and looking at items, consider the ease with which she can help dress herself. Easy-to-put-on clothes can save her — and you — a lot of frustration. If you choose clothes with big buttons or zippers and shoes with Velcro fasteners, you'll make it easier for her. Wide sleeves with big armholes and wide-necked garments will also help.

Coping with Fears

If your child is afraid of the noise of trains and trucks, toilet flushing, police sirens, or the vacuum cleaner, be patient with her.

She may have other fears. Whatever they are, they are real to her. Telling her it's "nothing to be afraid of" won't make it better. Accept the fears as the real feelings they are.

Gently help her cope. If she's afraid of the dark, for

example, provide a little night light. If she's fearful of storms, let her stay close to you until it's over. If you're not afraid, she probably will follow your example eventually.

Don't Rush Toilet Teaching

She's acting like she wants to go to the toilet by herself. She says, "Mama, pee pee."

Clancy Jane

Toilet teaching (training) is not an appropriate task for most children under two. Their brains and bodies have not matured enough yet. They simply are not ready. Efforts spent at toilet teaching a child too soon result mostly in frustration for parents and child.

For a discussion of toilet teaching, see *Discipline from Birth to Three*.

Major Tasks for Parents

As a parent of a child just learning to get around, you have three major tasks. First, you need to design your child's world so that she can satisfy her curiosity without getting hurt and without causing damage to your home. If you can child-proof your house or apartment and your yard, you'll be doing your child and yourself a favor.

Your second job is to react to your child when she wants you. She may want your help because she's frustrated at something she can't do herself. She may have hurt herself slightly and needs comforting. Or she may be excited and want you to share her excitement. Your assistance, comfort, and enthusiasm are important to her.

It's crucial to your child's learning that you respond promptly to her needs and to her interests. If you're talking on the phone, it's better to say, "I'm talking on the phone. I'll be with you in a minute," than it is to ignore her. Of course, you'll then need to be with her "in a minute."

Your third major responsibility with your child is to carry out your role as authority. Being firm is often necessary. Don't say "No" constantly, or you'll destroy some of your child's curiosity. When you do say "No," mean what you say.

If you say "No," then laugh because she looks pretty funny sitting in the middle of the dining table playing in the sugar bowl, will she take you seriously? Instead, say "No," get her down from the table, and put the sugar bowl away.

The important thing is to see that she carries out your requests. At this age, this generally means removing your child from the situation or distracting her. Ideally, you won't say "No" a second time because you'll already have taken care of the problem.

Most Important Stage in Life

Marty explores everything. He opens doors, closets, drawers, pulls all his clothes out. I just go in there and pick them up and make him help. It's not that drastic when a kid pulls his clothes out of his drawer. When he's old enough, he'll fold them up himself. Now he helps . . . he hands them to me.

Yumiko

Helping your toddler develop well is perhaps the greatest challenge you will ever face. How she develops socially and intellectually now is the basis for all of her future development in these areas. Her growth in language and curiosity during this time is of vital importance.

While parenting during this stage has many difficult times, you will also find lots of enjoyment in a well developing toddler. You will find you're no longer living with a baby but, rather, with a young and very interesting little person.

Enjoy your child!

Double the fun with twins.

3

12 - 24 Months

Active Play —
A Toddler's Work

- **Play *with* Your Child**
- **Active Play Is Valuable**
- **Play Ball!**
- **Play Space, Play Time Needed**
- **Play with Him Often**
- **Classifying Objects**
- **Plan for Indoor Play**
- **Making Toys at Home**

When I'm playing with him and I'm happy, he's happy.

Willadean, 17 - Rashad, 21 months

What I like about her is she's fun. She's real playful with almost everybody. You play with her just a little bit and she'll smile a lot. She always has a smile on her face. People say she looks like me.

I like taking her with me to the park when I go there with my friends to play handball.

Marcus, 16 - Liliane, 15 months

Meghan likes to figure things out. She loves things that are not toys, especially her father's tools and hammers. Of course she only plays with them when daddy is right beside her.

She loves to play with keys, to unlock the doors like mommy and daddy. She likes to play outside with the kids, but she still comes in often to check on me.

Louise, 19 - Meghan, 22 months; Mark, 5 months

Play *with* Your Child

I get on my knees and crawl with Meghan, and I chase her. I dance with her. I take her outside and play ball with her.

Louise

Playing with your child is important. He loves to play with you. As you play, stop occasionally to watch him without interrupting his play. You can learn a lot about the ways he likes to play. Let him lead you into playing at his level.

Building elaborate block structures while he watches is not exactly playing *with* him. He won't learn as much if he simply watches you as he will if he's actively playing.

During this time he will start holding things in both hands. He'll stack blocks on top of each other. Emptying and filling containers may keep him entertained for a considerable time.

As his language develops, ask him to talk about his play. What is he doing? If he's scribbling or coloring, ask him about his picture. Don't say, "What is that?" Instead, suggest, "Tell me about your drawing."

Remember that his attention span is still very short. When he decides to stop playing, respect his judgment.

Active Play Is Valuable

Trilby just started walking, and she's doing real good. She's real playful, always wanting to play.

I take her to the park and we play around. We put

her in the baby swing, and she loves it. I sing to her. I do everything I can.

Saunders, 17 - Trilby, 13 months

Running, climbing, jumping, swinging, and generally leaping about are all important for your toddler's development. Playground equipment can be exciting for her if it's not too large or elaborate and hard to use. If she can climb it herself, and if she wants to, she's probably safe, and will be able to get down by herself.

When I take Meghan to the park, she climbs. At first, she wanted me to come get her down from each thing, but I thought she should learn a little independence. I would sort of close my eyes and not help her for a while. It seemed mean, but I thought if I'm there to do it, she'll expect Mommy to help her all the time.

Louise

"Look, mom. I can drive!"

If you help her get up on the equipment, you may have to help her get down. Let her do as much as she can by herself.

Don't help her much, and don't urge her to play on something about which she feels fearful. Sometimes you may need to help her get down or simply remove her from equipment that is too dangerous.

Toddlers generally love to swing. Do you have a tree or something else to use for hanging a swing? An old tire on a strong rope makes a great swing. Some toddlers would rather be pushed in the swing than do almost anything else.

Luciann knows how to jump. She loves jumping on the bed. She likes jumping when she's happy. I let her jump on the bed when I'm holding her hands, but not by herself. She can jump on the floor all she wants.
                                        Liliana, 17 - Luciann, 22 months

Acrobatics are fun for toddlers. Is there any way you can let her play on an old crib mattress on the floor? Jumping on your bed can be pretty destructive and dangerous if she should fall off. If you have an old mattress or foam rubber pad you can put on the floor, she'll love playing on it.

Shelly is very active. She'll watch people do something, then try to copy them. My cousin does gymnastics, and she tries to do what he does.
                                        Dixie, 18 - Shelly, 17 months

If you don't have stairs in your home, find some occasionally so she can practice going up and down. Otherwise, with no practice in coming down safely, she's apt to fall when she's at the top of a flight of stairs.

Shelly is good at stairs now. She used to fall. She climbs them on her knees, then comes down on her butt. At first, it was a problem. When she was real

quiet, I'd know she was going upstairs. I let her go,
but I was right behind her.

Dixie

A smooth board (no splinters) about eight inches wide
and six feet long makes a good "toy." Your toddler can use
it for a balancing board. Putting one foot directly in front of
the other is a hard task for toddlers. She can practice on the
board. She can also practice this skill on the lines of your
floor tiles.

Walking the plank is even more fun if you set it up on
two low piles of magazines. An inch above the floor is
plenty high at first. Later, your child will be able to walk up
when one end is raised slightly.

She'll enjoy riding toys although she may not be ready
for a tricycle until she's at least two. Best is a low kiddy car
in which she can sit and push herself along with her feet.
You need to look for one that is simply built and won't
spread her legs too far apart. Remember that toddlers have
short legs. Some plastic cars are built too wide.

Competent as your toddler is, you still need *always* to
supervise water play, whether in the bathtub or outdoors.
She will continue to enjoy this kind of play, especially if
you join her. She may even be able to blow soap bubbles
very soon.

Remember, however, that a child can drown in an inch
of water. She should *never* be left alone with even a little
water in the tub or play pool.

Play Ball!

We play ball. I throw the ball, the dog picks it up,
and brings it to me, puts it down. Todd then picks it up
and throws it.

We always play chase in the house. I act like I'm a

monster and I'm going to get him. He loves it.

Jill, 18 - Todd, 16 months

*Sean throws a big ball and kicks it. He's been
playing with it for about two weeks. He has a smaller
one that he throws around and kicks, too.*

Ginger, 18 - Sean, 17 months

Sometime after her first birthday, she will enjoy simple
ball games. By the time she's two, she may be able to
throw overhand more or less in your direction. She can kick
a ball, too.

A tennis ball can provide a lot of fun for a toddler. She
can have a wonderful time throwing it and watching it
bounce. It's easier for her to handle than is a bigger ball.

He and Mom have a good time playing together.

Perhaps best of all, she's less likely to knock a lamp over, put out a window, or hurt another child with a tennis ball.

She picks up everything. She tries to play baseball. She'll hit it and do the running. She always slides into base. She's a real character.

Darla, 17 - Janis, 2

Play Space, Play Time Needed

Tatiana likes toys that make a lot of noise, that ring, that talk to her. She likes the telephone more than anything. We have this phone where we can push the button and it sounds like it's ringing. We tell her to answer the phone.

When I'm talking to someone, she thinks I'm talking to her, and she answers back on her phone. She has a little plastic slide in her room. She likes to play on it, but not as much as she likes going outside.

Mihaela, 16 - Tatiana, 18 months

Wherever you live, even if it's a crowded apartment, try to make play space for your toddler. It's still best if this space can be part of the kitchen or living room close to you rather than in a room away from everyone.

Organizing your child's play materials is important. If he can't find part of the toy he wants, he won't play as well. Does he seem to have lots of toys that he doesn't use? Are some of them broken? Are there parts missing? Are they hard to find at the bottom of a deep toy box? Are they hidden behind storage doors?

Perhaps you can get a few open shelves. Concrete blocks and boards, if not stacked too high, make good shelving. Make sure they are stable so your toddler can't push them down. Help him keep his big toys on the bottom shelf, his others where he can reach them.

It's wise to have only a few toys readily available, the toys he's really interested in at the time. When you bring his other toys out again, they may seem new and interesting. If you leave everything out, a child this age will simply throw them all over the floor. You may even want him to use the more complicated stacking toys only at times when you can play with him.

Roseanna, 14, and Felipe, 2, lived in a small apartment with little storage space. Roseanna placed several hooks high on the wall. On each hook she hung a pillowcase of toys. They came down for play one at a time.

The apartment was less of a disaster area, and Felipe's play undoubtedly was more satisfying to him. He wasn't confused by seeing all his toys dumped out at once.

Mihaela mentioned a similar tactic. She switches toys daily for Tatiana, keeping some in the closet and putting others out for her use.

Play With Him Often

Jamaica likes to read books. She likes puzzles and blocks, and loves her dolls.

She likes to get in the tub with me. She loves to play in the water. Just being around each other makes us more happy.

Kyli, 17 - Jamaica, 22 months

I love this age when Derek is running around. It makes me feel good that I can teach him something.

After dinner he starts winding up again, so I usually take him for a walk. He wants to know what everything is. By the time we get back, he's pretty calm again.

Laurette, 17 - Derek, 18 months

Laurette is a wise mother. Taking Derek for a walk when he's "wound up" is much better for both of them, far better than his mother insisting he "Calm down right now!" In addition, chances are good that Derek will be ready for bed after he's had his walk with his mom.

Play with your child regularly. Hopefully, you'll do this because you want to. Of course your work and activities take a lot of time, and they — and you — are very important. But if he has to whine and beg to get your attention, the ten minutes of play you finally give him won't be much fun for either of you. Remember, too, that you can "play" with him while you're working:

> *Luciann hides underneath the cupboard and I say, "I'm going to get you." She loves it.*
> *She likes to go into the kitchen and play with pots and pans. She only goes in there when I'm around.*
>
> Liliana

Make the most of whatever time you can give your child. Be sure to give him your full attention. Follow his lead. Does he want to roll a ball back and forth? Then play ball with him.

Tomorrow he may decide to let you help him build a tower with his blocks, or perhaps he'll be ready to finger paint. Always talk to him about whatever you're doing together.

Bowling Game

Use half-gallon milk cartons for bowling pins. You may need to put blocks or sand inside them to give them enough stability to stand up. Then show your child how to roll a ball toward the "pins" to try to knock them over.

A follow-the-leader game is easy to organize right in your living room. You be the leader first. You might crawl under the table, around a chair, through a big box you've placed there, and over the big ball beside the box. Next time, let your child be the leader.

Throwing newspaper balls is fun for a toddler and remarkably safe for your house. Crumple newspaper into a ball and hold it together with a little tape. Make several and offer them to your child.

If he's naming small objects such as a ball, a car, a spoon, and a doll, make him a feel-box. A box in which small appliances are shipped is usually sturdy enough for this game. Cut a hole in the side big enough for your child's hand.

Show him the little items one at a time. Let him handle and examine them. Then put each one inside the box. Ask him to put his hand in the box and pick up an item. Then, without taking it out or looking at it, ask him to tell you what it is.

Classifying Objects

You may notice your toddler is beginning to sort items into groups. This is a start toward making sense out of his world by classifying things and people into categories. He has already classified people into those he knows and trusts and those he doesn't. He certainly classifies toys into "mine" and, more slowly, "yours."

When you purchase toys for him, a good set of small objects is a good buy. Be sure none of the parts are so small that he could choke on them. Perhaps you'll choose a city street scene or a barn with animals and people.

You'll find he begins playing by classifying — dividing the people from the animals, for example. Soon he will be creating scenes and using his imagination. He'll make the cars go fast, the dogs chase one another, and the policemen stop traffic.

Another "game" idea — suggest she sort the laundry or her clothes by color.

Plan for Indoor Play

Casey is very busy now, into everything. He's happy — he thinks he's the funniest person in the world, and I agree with him!

He's starting to learn movements to songs. He dances, and I dance with him. I turn on the radio and dance with him.

Painting outside means less mess inside.

He's learning a lot right now. He's learning new words. I sing the alphabet to him.

Charity, 17 - Casey, 18 months

Scribbling has been called the art of the toddler. Scribbling is how she learns to draw. Instead of teaching her to draw later, show her how to scribble during her second

year. Her scribbling will turn into drawing a year or so
from now.

> *She's very good with crayons. I put her at the table*
> *— with the paint. Her clothes are all stained with*
> *paint. I try to let her be a kid, enjoy herself.*
>   Clancy Jane, 17 - Jenae, 25 months

Putting out big sheets of paper for painting and scribbling is important. You don't have to buy paper. Just put in
front of your child big paper bags that have been cut open.
(Ask for paper instead of plastic bags when you buy
groceries.) First, you put a mark on the paper with an over-
sized kindergarten crayon. Then hand the crayon to her,
saying, "Now you color." She will love it. She will also
need supervision unless you want the scribbling extended
to your walls, furniture, and telephone book. For more
about this, see *Discipline from Birth to Three.*

It's time to make or buy a few simple puzzles for your
child. Paste a picture on cardboard, then cut it in three
pieces. Can she fit them together? If she does it quickly,
perhaps she's ready for a harder task. If so, cut the same
puzzle into five or six pieces. Can she still put it together?

She can probably place a circle and a square in a
formboard. You can make one for her by drawing a big
square and circle on a piece of cardboard, then filling each
one in with a different color. Cut out the same size square
and circle from white paper. Color the shapes to match
those on the cardboard. Can she match them yet?

Making Toys at Home

She may be able to string large "beads" now. The beads
can be empty spools, empty tape rollers, or even hair
rollers. Dip about two inches of the end of some cord in
white glue. Let it dry, and it will be stiff enough for your

toddler to stick it through the holes. The cord should be no longer than ten inches. You don't want to run the risk of her wrapping the cord around her neck.

A few months ago, your child probably learned to stack one block on top of another. Now she can make a higher stack, a tower of blocks. Or she may stack cans of food, one on top of the other.

> *Lance climbs right into the cupboards with the pots and pans. Then he puts them inside each other. He can play in the lower cupboards although I rubber-banded one that I don't want him into.*
>
> *He gets out the pans and bangs them together. He also bangs the cupboard doors back and forth.*
>
> Celia, 20 - Laurel, 4; Lance, 18 months

She will enjoy rearranging all kinds of objects around the house. She may take everything out of your kitchen cupboard and line the items up on the floor. She may balk at putting them away. If the job seems too much for her, ask her to help you put them back. Perhaps she'd like to sort them by color or size. Then you'd say, "Let's put all the big ones away first." Or make a game of seeing if she can put them away as fast as you put lunch on the table.

Play is your child's work. Through play, she learns more about her world. Joining in her play is an important part of building a good relationship with her. Time spent playing with her is likely to mean less time spent solving problems she causes because of boredom or lack of attention.

Most important, you and your toddler can enjoy each other tremendously!

She has a marvelous time pretending.

4

Her Imagination Soars

- **She Loves to Pretend**
- **Let Him "Help"**
- **Toddlers and Talking**
- **Don't Correct His Speech**
- **Read to Your Child**
- **Choose Non-Sexist Books**
- **You're the Teacher**

She wants to do everything I do. When I take a shower with her I put the shampoo in my hair and start washing it. She will do the same thing.

Everything that I say she repeats. If I say, "Excuse me, young lady," she will say the same thing. When I do my hair, when I put makeup on my face, she'll watch me. Then a little later she will grab my makeup and do it exactly the way I did.

Clancy Jane, 17 - Jenae, 25 months

Leon pretends he's a dog, a cat, a bird flying. Sometimes he rides a horse (on the arm of the couch).

He and DeeDee will go in the bedroom and pretend
they're in outer space. They will sit and talk and talk.
He understands her and she understands him.

Tamara, 21 - DeeDee, 41/2; Leon, 20 months

She Loves to Pretend

Janis does a lot of acting. I got sample diapers in
the mail the other day. She went in and got them and
said, "These are for me. The mailman sent them for
me." She asked me to put them on her, so I did. Then
she pretended she was a baby and crawled around.

She likes music a lot, punk rock. She sees my broth-
er pretend like he's playing a guitar, so she does, too.

Darla, 17 - Janis, 2

Often children in this age group have a marvelous time
pretending. They love to dress up in mother's or daddy's
clothes.

Putting on your shoes may be a favorite activity for him.
Different kinds of hats will fascinate him. Save some of
your old clothes for his dress-up play.

Antonio plays house with his cowboys, soldiers,
and boats. He loves motorcycles — the little ones and
the real ones. We went by the shop yesterday, and he
wanted to get on one.

He will tell his doll "No," which is what I tell him.
Or he'll say, "Behave yourself."

Becky, 18 - Antonio, 26 months

Soon your child may involve you in her make-believe
play. If she invites you to feed her teddy bear, do so. Your
participation is good for her, and besides, you'll have fun.

She carries her baby around. We got her a little
stroller and she thinks she's the mom. She puts a

towel over her baby and pats the baby. She has a little
rocking chair and she rocks her baby.

Liliana, 17 - Luciann, 22 months

Dolls are important to almost all children. Most parents
now seem to understand boys need dolls as much as girls
do. After all, if playing with dolls is early practice toward
being a parent, it must be as important for boys as for girls.
Most men, as well as most women, will become parents.

Janet has two dolls, a boy doll and a bear doll,
Frankie and Henry. She takes them in the tub with
her. She calls them her babies and takes them to bed.

Candi, 16 - Janet, 18 months

Most toddlers love music. Music stimulates brain development because the child hears it, moves with it, and may
sing with it. She may
turn the radio on so
she'll have music for
her dancing. Dance
with her if she asks
you. You'll both
enjoy it. She'd like
her own musical
instrument such as a
drum, cymbals, or
musical triangle. You
can make her a drum
from a one-pound
coffee can. Two pan
lids make cymbals.

Toddlers love
bells. You have to
supervise two or
more toddlers ringing

Today she's a musician.

bells because in their exuberance they might hit each other.
It's worth the effort, however.

Let Him "Help"

Henry will open the drawer and get a can opener.
Then he'll get a can and give it to me, or he'll try to
open the can himself. He likes to do what I do. He can
even unlock the front door himself. We have to watch
him constantly.

Olivia, 20 - Henry, 23 months

Toddlers generally love to "help" with the housework. If
he can have a small broom, he'll sweep right along with
you. Mopping the floor with a rag is his idea of real play.

When you're cooking, you can think of ways to involve
him. Let him add the seasonings, pre-measured by you, of
course. If you're baking, he can help you stir the mixture.

If you can figure a way to let him help you wash dishes
without having a nervous breakdown yourself, he'll love it.
If you have two sinks, he can use one to wash plastic
spoons, cups, plates, and pans. You'll probably be ahead if
you put a lot of newspapers on the floor before he starts
washing dishes. Then his spills can be rolled up and thrown
away. Or put bath towels on the floor to catch the water.

Sometimes even a shopping trip with your toddler can be
fun for both of you:

I think she enjoys shopping as much as I do. We go
together, and I talk to her. I'll say, "Jenae, do you
like this?" Whatever I do, she does.

Clancy Jane

He can be a real help at times. He can follow your
simple request, "Bring me the dustcloth." He can help you
make the beds, especially his own. He will love to
mimic you.

Toddlers and Talking

You've been helping your child learn to speak ever since she was born. You've talked to her, named things and people, read to her. She may be saying quite a few words now.

> *Sean knows his body parts — nose, eyes, mouth, ears, hands, feet, legs. He just learned his arms yesterday. He answers the telephone. He says, "Who's this?" and then keeps talking.*
>
> Ginger, 18 - Sean, 17 months

If there are words you don't want your toddler to learn, try not to have those words said when she's around. She's learning to talk by repeating the words she hears. Punishing a child for using "bad" words doesn't make much sense. To the child, all the words she hears are interesting, and she should not be expected to censor her own speech for several years.

He's saying a few words. Soon he'll be talking.

An infant center teacher talked about a two-year-old whose language was outrageous. "We didn't make a big deal of it," she reported. "We ignored the word. We went on as if he didn't say it. We would distract him to something else. Sometimes we'd comment in a matter-of-fact way, 'Oh, we don't use that word.' Then we'd go on to another activity. Gradually his language improved."

Don't Correct His Speech

Now that he's beginning to say a few words, there are two more ways you can help him.

First, don't correct his speech. When you talk to him, pronounce the words correctly and clearly. But if he says "pitty" for "pretty," don't worry about it. He'll learn faster if you don't criticize.

Second, your child may not bother talking if he sees no need to do so. If he points at the refrigerator, do you immediately hand him a cup of juice? If he gestures for a cracker, do you give it to him right now? Instead, try encouraging him to say the word when possible. Don't frustrate him, of course, by waiting more than a few seconds. Remember that children start talking at different ages.

Shelly pulls at me to get attention. She says "Bottle" and "Eat." If she wants something, she calls it out. She's been doing that for about two months.
                                    Dixie, 18 - Shelly, 17 months

Jayme says "Mommy," "Daddy," "No," "Yes," "Grandma," and especially, "What's this?" He's pretty curious about everything.

He responds when I talk with him. We can actually carry on a conversation.
                                    Kaylene, 18 - Jayme, 16 months

While most children can name familiar things and occasionally speak in two-word phrases toward the end of the second year, your perfectly bright two-year-old may say scarcely a word. Don't worry about it. Continue talking to him about the things you're doing with him. Use simple, clear, slow speech. By the end of this stage, your child may be talking in "sentences." His version of a sentence, however, is generally one word such as "Hi." If he says "Up," he means "Pick me up." Don't expect sentences complete with a noun, a verb, and an object. Most children don't speak in real sentences until after their second birthday.

Book of _____'s Words

Use light cardboard for the pages. The cardboard in panty hose packages works well. Punch holes in the pages and tie them together with yarn. Find pictures to represent the words your child is saying. "Ma-ma," "Da-da," "Bye," and "Dog" may be his first understandable words. Put a picture of each in the book, then read it with him. Soon he may be "reading" the pictures to you.

Read to Your Child

If you've been reading to your child, he's probably talking more than he would have otherwise.

I read to Shelly. I think that helps her learn to talk. I started reading to her when she was ten months old.

I don't like to read unless it's what I want to read. But when I read to Shelly, I know what I'm getting out of it. I enjoy it. And she starts mumbling as though she's reading. That's how she learned the name doggie, etc. She turns the pages herself.

Dixie

Sean takes a book, opens it up, and jabbers like
he's reading. I read to him a lot. He likes to point at
the pictures, and he listens when I read to him.

Ginger

The pictures are the important thing. Don't get hung up
on teaching your child to read for several years yet. You
can count on him learning to read with less struggle later if
he enjoys books with you now. When you choose books
for your toddler, you'll want those with bright, simple
pictures. At this age, his favorites probably are books with
pictures of things
and people he
already knows
about.

Heidi
loves picture
books. I read
to her. She
has books in
her toy box.
She looks at
them, then
shows me
and grunts
that she
wants me to
read to her.
It's really
amazing how
she wants to
talk so bad.

Jenny, 18 -
Heidi, 13 months

Reading with Mom is a special time.

If her grandparents live with or near you, a book about a child playing with Grampa will interest her. Books about dogs and cats are good. She may especially like stories with pictures of babies.

As she grows older, of course, you won't limit her books to stories about familiar things. The rhythm of Mother Goose rhymes will appeal to her. Fairy tales and stories about animals, people, and places she has never seen are an important part of her education. Provide lots of variety in her books, because books can widen her knowledge of and interest in many different things. Books about familiar topics, however, are more likely to keep a toddler's interest.

Choose Non-Sexist Books

Books can play an important part in a child's learning about himself and his world. Don't let his books show a slanted, sexist picture of the world. Too often, children's picture books portray most mothers in the kitchen cooking dinner and fathers out earning the living.

Look for books that show boys and girls, men and women, as human beings with lots of different abilities and interests. Don't choose stories and illustrations that suggest that your child must limit his/her interests because of his/her sex.

You're the Teacher

As you read to your child and encourage the development of his imagination, you're laying the foundation for reading and other successful school experiences for him later. In fact, you are your child's most important teacher. He will learn far more interacting with you during this stage than he ever will again.

This is an exciting time for both of you!

Both Dad and toddler win if Dad's involved.

5

Dad's Ahead
If He's Involved

- **Some Fathers
  Are Very Involved**
- **Others Leave It
  Up to Mom**
- **Building a Family**
- **Learning
  to Be a Father**
- **When Dad
  Lives Elsewhere**
- **Maintaining
  a Relationship**
- **Your Child
  Changes Your Life**

I didn't plan it. I didn't expect the pregnancy. We decided to live together after Kamie was born. I want to be in her life because my dad wasn't there for me. I want to see the little things she does. I want to help her, guide her. She's my daughter and I love her.

Parenting is one of the hardest things I've ever experienced. She wakes you up, "I'm hungry, change me, dress me." She loves attention. There are other things I want to do that I can't. It's hard. I do everything. I change her, I feed her, I bathe her. I want to do everything.

Lucas, 21 - Kamie, 21 months

A lot of fathers don't live with their kid. They just
come in and visit on weekends or after school, while I
can see Alex all the time. I saw him when he started
walking, and when he first said "Daddy." That makes
me more involved with him.

Alex made me less selfish in a way that I just can't
go out and get everything for me. I have to consider
that he needs this, he gets that.

I have a lot to share with him. Like now I'm trying
to teach him to catch a ball. I'm like every other
father in wanting him to be a baseball star, and I want
to get him out there young.

I didn't expect to have a baby this young. I hadn't
planned on it until I was 25 when I would be stable
and set and it was time to have kids. It just happened.

Brian, 20 - Alex, 12 months

Some Fathers Are Very Involved

Teen mothers or fathers who parent alone often have to
learn how to take complete responsibility for caring for
their child(ren). More often it's the teen mother who cares
for the child if the parents aren't together. No matter how
tired she is, she's the one who feeds him, plays with him,
takes care of him when he's sick, and performs all the other
parenting tasks because she's the live-in parent. As a result,
she develops a strong bond with her child. She experiences
the joys of parenting as well as the hard work.

Ideally, if the parents live together, they share child care
responsibilities. More and more fathers are realizing how
much better their relationship with their child is if they're
deeply involved in caring for that child. They know that if
only mom takes care of the baby, dad misses out.

I'm as involved in Dustin's life as Kelly Ellen is.
We both share everything with him. I've felt real

attached since the moment he was born.

We both read to him. Books are his favorite now. Everywhere we go he's got to have books. He has his favorites.

In sports, you learn everything you can to be the best you can be. I feel that way about him. I want him to be brought up the best way we can.

Every day is a different day with him. Every day we learn something, whether it's his personality change or something we learn from another child in another family.

I take care of Dustin because I love him. If I didn't love him, I wouldn't be here. He's part of me, and I want to be with him and bring him up.

Mark, 22 - Dustin, 2½

Sometimes "Dad" is not the child's biological (real) father. Perhaps mom is with someone else, someone who plays the father role to her child, Mom may already know the acting dad, the one who loves her child and takes daily responsibility for him, is the truly "real" father.

If your partner is not your child's father, how involved should he be in child care? That depends on a lot of things. If you're developing a strong relationship, and you expect to be together for a long time, he will probably want to be quite involved with your child.

Leesha's real close to Greg. Even though he isn't her natural father, he's her father. Like when I was pregnant with Manuel, Greg would get up in the middle of the night when Leesha needed him. He's the one who picks her up from school. That's a father, someone who is there for her, who feeds her and bathes her, not someone who made her.

Kambria, 21 - Leesha, 5; Manuel, 14 months

However, it's always best to be honest with your toddler. Even if she never sees her biological father, she needs to know she has another dad.

Others Leave It Up to Mom

Dads do indeed play an important role in a child's life. Some fathers, however, even if they live with their children, leave the child care up to mom.

> *Dennis isn't too much help, perhaps because of the problems we've had. He thinks the baby is just mine. His mom helps me a lot, and my mom did when I lived at home. You can get very irritable if you don't have anybody to help you.*
>
> Jenny, 18 - Heidi, 13 months

Louise expressed that irritability forcefully:

> *Bob isn't always here, and when he is, he isn't that much help. Last night I blew up at him. When he gets home, I like to sit down and relax. So I went next door to visit a friend.*
>
> *As soon as one of the kids says "Boo," he comes over and gets me. I asked him, "Can't I ever leave this house to take a break without having you coming after me, or Meghan tagging along?"*
>
> *If he goes out that door to visit some of the guys in the complex here, I'm not to bother him. It seems like mother is supposed to do everything with the kids.*
>
> Louise, 19 - Mark, 5 months; Meghan, 23 months

Mick didn't expect to change his daughter's diapers and feed her, perhaps because he didn't live with her until she was 14 months old. In fact, Kris continued doing these tasks for several months after they moved in with Mick and his family. Then Kris got a weekend job, and Mick discovered he had no choice:

> *When Kris and Cassandra moved in with us, I didn't think I'd be taking care of Cassie. Then Kris started working weekends, so I have Cassie all day Saturday and Sunday. At first I'd say, "Mom, change her."*
>
> *She would say, "No, you do it."*
>
> *Or I'd tell my sisters to change her.*
>
> *"No, it's your kid," they would tell me. I had no choice.*
>
> *Now I feed her and play with her a lot. We play basketball. I take her to the park and we play kickball.*
>
> Mick, 19 - Cassandra, 25 months

She's helping Dad read.

Mick undoubtedly has a much closer bonding with
Cassandra now that he is sharing her care.

Building a Family

If you're the dad, how much time do you spend with
your child? Do you do your share of diaper changing and
bath-giving? Do you play with him now, or are you waiting
until he's big enough to play football with you? If you're
the mother, do you assume you should be the one to be
with your toddler most of the time? Or would you like dad,
if he's with you, to get more involved?

Ernesta felt very strongly that mother and father should
share child care. She understood the benefits not only to
herself, but for the baby and the father. Osvaldo didn't
agree at first, but Ernesta didn't give up her dream of a
family with both parents involved with their children:

> *At first when the baby needed changing, my hus-
> band would say, "No, that's the mother's job."*
>
> *I'd say, "No, it's not just the mother's job. I didn't
> have the baby by myself. It took both of us."*
>
> *In the beginning he wouldn't help. We fought a lot
> about that. Finally I told his mom that he didn't want
> to help me do anything. His mom got mad at him and
> told him, "You have to help her."*
>
> *My father never helped my mom, so I grew up
> without any idea of how to talk to my dad. I told
> Osvaldo, "If you want a relationship like that, forget
> it. We'll just end our relationship right here. I want a
> family where the father is very involved." That made
> him think about it.*
>
> *We even went to see a counselor once, and she
> helped us a lot. Now he helps me, and I think it's
> great. I think all fathers should, not just because*

*mothers need help, but because he has to build a
relationship with the baby himself. There's mother
love and father love, not just mother love for the baby.*

Ernesta, 20 - Jeremy, 3; Osvaldo, Jr., 5 months

Osvaldo now has a better relationship with his children
because of Ernesta's insistence that he share the child care.

Learning to Be a Father

Meghan, too, was convinced that parenting is for mothers *and* fathers. Her father was never at home as she was
growing up. Tim's parents played the traditional roles of
dad out working and mom home with the kids.

Meghan wanted more for their children. She and Tim
didn't marry until Angel was nearly two. In fact, they split
up during pregnancy, and Tim didn't see his son until
Angel was five months old. From that time on, he spent a
lot of time with Meghan and Angel. Meghan shared
their story:

*I said Tim didn't need to be with me but I wanted
our son to know him. He started coming over, and he
started playing daddy real quick. I showed him how to
change diapers. I said, "You need to be part of his
life. I'll show you how to change a diaper. You'll
catch on, you will."*

*He was scared. He didn't know how to take care of
Angel. He would always ask me what to do, and I
said, "You're his father. You have to learn these
things."*

*Once when Angel needed a bath, and I told Tim to
do it, he said "No."*

I said, "Why not?"

"My father never gave me a bath."

I asked him to leave. He got me upset, and I didn't

*want to be upset in front of Angel because I knew a
baby gets upset if you're upset. Tim asked why I
wanted him to leave.*

*I said, "You're his father and I'm his mother, and I
thought we were in this 50-50. These are not the old
days. Maybe your father didn't give you a bath, does
that mean you can't bathe Angel? This is a whole
different situation. Maybe you had a bad childhood,
but don't take it out on Angel."*

He looked at me and said, "You're right again."

*I said, "Don't be scared. I'll be there to help you.
Nothing can happen except get him clean."*

*So we worked past that one, and he started giving
Angel baths. Then he started doing just about everything. His family has the old traditions. The mother is
in the kitchen and she's pregnant. She takes care of
the kids and daddy doesn't do anything with the kids.
They kind of resented that I got Tim to change.*

*We agreed that whatever we do is our business.
We're a family now, so whatever they think, they can
keep their opinions to themselves.*

Meghan, 25 - Angel, 8; Kenny, 6; Jose, 2; Leon, 8 months

Keeping up with a super-active toddler is hard. As
Meghan understood so well, if two parents can share the
child care, everyone will be better off. Mother won't get so
exhausted, daddy will enjoy his child more if he's involved,
and baby, of course, will be most pleased of all.

When Dad Lives Elsewhere

Some couples stay together throughout pregnancy, but
don't get married. Many break up after the baby is born. In
fact, the majority of teenage parents, whether or not they
marry, are not together by the time their child is three, or

She needs time with her dad.

even two years old.

Many, like Yumiko and Marc, never live together. During the early months of parenting, the couple may see a great deal of each other, but their relationship eventually ends. Where does dad fit in at this point?

Yumiko and Marc attended different high schools. Marc was working, but he saw Yumiko nearly every day during her pregnancy. For another year they remained close. He spent most evenings with Yumiko and Marty.

As the months went by, Yumiko realized she was growing up faster than Marc. They started fighting and finally split. Yumiko is seeing another man now. She described Marc's relationship with Marty:

> *Marc doesn't take much responsibility for Marty. I used to push him when we were together. I'd say, "You're a father now. You should do this."*

Now he doesn't come to see Marty very often.
Several times he's called and said he was coming
over to take Marty somewhere, and then he doesn't
show up. That was disappointing for Marty. I don't
feel there is any big reason for Marty to go over there.

I think Marc feels he doesn't have to worry about
seeing Marty because he'll always have some legal
rights. I don't like the idea of him showing up when
Marty is five and saying, "Hello, I'm your daddy." I
think it's unfair to a kid for daddy to show up just
when he feels like it.

Sometimes I feel like saying, "Go do your own
thing, Marc. Don't even come over here." I can't do
that, but I would think he could stop by here at least
once a week. Marty was used to seeing him every day.
He calls Marc "Daddy," but he doesn't really know
what that means.

Yumiko, 16 - Marty, 21 months

Marc is losing out the most in this situation. He's not
building a good relationship with Marty. In fact, it won't be
a relationship at all if he continues ignoring his little boy.

Leila is no longer with Larissa's father. They split while
Leila was pregnant, then lived together for six months after
the baby was born. Then he moved out of state. A few
months later he came back. Leila reported:

I'm not with Larissa's father any longer. Stewart
was coming in and out of her life, but now she's old
enough to be hurt by that. He's avoiding me now
because I filed for paternity, and he's not
cooperating.

When he came back to town the last time, I let
Larissa stay with him a couple of times. Then all of a
sudden he quit coming around, and I was left to

answer her questions about Daddy.

I've decided if Stewart does come around, it's going to have to be a legal decision. My daughter doesn't need that, someone coming in and out of her life. I'd give anything for her to have a dad, but if he's just going to hurt her . . .

Leila, 18 - Larissa, 2 1/2

It's a dilemma. Leila would like to protect Larissa from being hurt by her father's only-occasional visits. On the other hand, will Larissa feel even more abandoned by her father if she doesn't see him at all?

Each family is different, but every effort needs to be made to help Stewart understand how disappointing it is to his daughter when he goes in and out of her life. Even if a child doesn't live with her father, she needs to know he's there and he cares about her.

Leila is wise to file for paternity. Otherwise, Larissa might not qualify for support from Stewart. Neither would she have a legal right to such important things from him as possible veteran's or Social Security benefits.

Maintaining a Relationship

Many fathers who don't live with their children want a strong relationship with them. Marcus is an example:

Last night when Dorene came over, I was going out. All my friends were outside waiting for me, and here comes the mom with the baby. So I told my friends to go on because I was going to stay with my baby. At first I was disappointed because I wanted to go out with my friends. Then Liliane ran toward me smiling, and I knew I wanted to stay with her. My baby comes first, although sometimes it's hard.

Marcus, 16 - Liliane, 15 months

Miguel lived with his daughter's mother for several
months after Genny was born. In fact, if he had his way, he
would still be living with his family. Since that's not
possible, he spends as much time with Genny as he can:

*I'll continue to keep Genny whenever I can and buy
her things she needs. If I go shopping, it's not me I
have on my mind, it's them, and I'll buy them
something.*

*Today I didn't go to work, so I kept Genny all day.
She's not only my daughter — she's like a little friend.
I was playing with her all day. She's all active. She
gets me tired, but I love her so much I'd do anything
for her.*

*She goes in all the rooms, and I have to be alert.
She's smart. She does things I wouldn't think she
would do. I'll tell her to go get me a diaper. She'll do
it, and I'll give her a hug. Every time she does
something good, I hug her.*

Miguel, 20 - Genny, 18 months

Your Child Changes Your Life

Miguel also talked about the changes he has made in his
life because of his daughter:

*Maurine, Genny, and I lived together about six
months. It was good. I worked long hours, and then I
would see Genny. Sometimes I even worked on weekends, but when I didn't, I spent all my time with her.*

*Whenever you think you want to leave your wife or
your girlfriend, think about your child, and how you
want her to grow up. I care about myself, but I would
do anything for her. Don't ever be mean to her or
neglect her, just love her, and when she gets older,
she will give the love back to you.*

I used to be in a gang, but it feels better not being with the guys. I don't have many friends around here any more because they're all in the gangs. If you're older, it's not hard to get out of the gang. Me, I just walked away. No gang has ever had control over me. I was pressured into drugs, but not to shoot this guy or that guy. All the younger guys are like that now. I don't want to be like that. I decided to stay off the gangs.

I feel good about myself now. I used to be real heavy into drugs. I stopped as soon as I started trying to get back with Maurine. I changed right away because I figured who would want someone using drugs and with the gang? There's no use getting back to her if you're going to do all that.

We fought too much. We were getting along, but I was getting jealous a lot. I don't know why. Then she decided to move out. It's different now. We're friends, and I'll continue being as close to Genny as I can.

Miguel

Having a child drastically changes the lives of fathers as well as mothers. Yes, a father can walk away, and some fathers do just that. Other fathers, like Miguel, know that dad, as well as mother, will be ahead if he truly shares the parenting responsibilities along with the joys of rearing his child. Whether or not you live with your child, the more involved you are in his life, the better your relationship will be.

Your child needs you.

She prefers to feed herself.

6

Mealtime for Toddlers

- **Keeping Mealtime Pleasant**
- **She Can Eat with You**
- **Offer Small Helpings**
- **Coping with Messiness**
- **Toddler Needs Less Food**
- **Serving New Foods**
- **Outlaw Junk Food**
- **Fat-Proofing Your Toddler**
- **Nutrition/Extended Family Living**
- **It's Your Responsibility**

If Rashad wants food, he'll go to the refrigerator and point to what he wants. He loves fruit.

He eats entirely table food — I started giving him little bits of table food when he was about nine months old. He didn't much like baby food.

Willadean, 17 - Sal, 21 months

They still like me to feed them sometimes although most of the time they feed themselves.

They have to have the exact same food or the other one will start taking the first one's food, and she'll get mad.

Edie - twins Dora and Laura, 26 months

Keeping Mealtime Pleasant

Many adults consider eating an enjoyable pastime. Some of us enjoy it too much! But for many small children, mealtime becomes a hassle, a fight with mother and dad.

"Eat your meat right now."

"Just one more bite of green beans."

"No dessert for you until you finish your carrots!"

A toddler's mealtime doesn't have to be a bad experience for everyone. Toddlers have the same kinds of food needs as the rest of us. They need nutritious foods from each of the food groups (milk and other dairy products, fruits, vegetables, bread and cereals, protein foods). They also need a relaxed, friendly atmosphere at mealtime. Both needs are important, as Esteban points out:

> *Nathan eats pretty good. He likes vegetables. I used to get all nervous trying to feed him, and it seems to me the kid knows when you're nervous, and you just get more nervous. Instead, you want to make it fun while they eat.*
>
> Esteban, 18 - Nathan, 2; Ralph, 5 months

She Can Eat With You

By now, your child can probably eat her meals with you. With a little planning, most of your easy-to-chew food should be suitable for her. Cut meat, fish, and vegetables into bite-size cubes, pieces she can pick up with her fingers.

If you're frying food for your family, it's better for your toddler if you broil or dry-fry her food in a non-stick pan. Serve her food before you add the spices or the rich sauce. Foods to avoid completely at this age include popcorn and nuts or any food that might cause her to choke.

> *Susie eats everything in sight. She's a little pig. She's never been finicky. I think it's because everyone*

*else eats everything. We never had a problem with her
eating. We don't let her drink a lot of soda, and she's
allergic to milk, so we give her the Lactaid which is a
liquid she drinks with every meal.*

*She often eats two helpings of dinner. She loves
hamburger. Food has never been a battle, and I think
that has a lot to do with grandma. Up here we don't
have that many fast-food places, so we do a lot of
home cooking.*

Cathi, 18 - Susie, 34 months

Convenience foods such as canned soups are not as
nutritious as foods you prepare yourself. Soups and other
dehydrated meals usually contain more salt than your child
should have. These foods also contain a variety of preserva-
tives, colorings, and artificial flavorings. It's all right to
serve them occasionally, but a steady diet of already-
prepared foods is not especially good for any of us. Neither
is a steady diet of fast-foods.

Offer Small Helpings

Give her small helpings of food. Don't worry if she
doesn't seem to eat much. She doesn't need as much as she
did six months ago when she was growing so much faster
than she is now. She needs daily:

- Twenty ounces of milk (21/2 cups)
- Fruits and vegetables
- Bread and cereal
- Protein foods

If she doesn't drink enough milk, put it in puddings and
soups. Does she like cheese? Let cheese take the place of
some of her milk. Cottage cheese and yogurt are also good
replacements.

While most toddlers insist on feeding themselves, you

may find she occasionally insists just as strongly that you
feed her. That's all right. She may not be feeling well, or
she may simply be tired of feeding herself all the time.

Allow plenty of time for your toddler to eat. Rushing
through a meal is not her style. She'll eat many foods with
her fingers, but by her second birthday, she'll be able to
handle a spoon quite well.

Coping with Messiness

When Derek eats and he's through, he's through.

*You'd better
get him down
fast — or
he'll throw
his food and
jump out of
his high
chair!*

Laurette, 17 -
Derek, 18
months

Learning to use
a spoon is hard
work and takes a
lot of practice. He
has to try. If
mother insists on
neatness at the
table, he'll be
discouraged. While
he's learning, it's
impossible for him
to be neat.

*Toddlers do **not** eat neatly!*

When he eats a cracker, he may first gum it. Then he'll rub the mess all over his face and into his hair. There is no reason to let him sit on the couch while he makes this mess, of course, but his high chair can be cleaned up.

Put a thick layer of newspapers on the floor under his chair to catch the spills. Roll them up after dinner and throw them away. Then you have only your toddler and his chair to clean. He is fairly easily washed, although he may not appreciate your efforts. If you give him a second washcloth to use on himself while you clean him up, it may help. Try not to let the mess upset you.

Some parents are so horrified at the mess their toddler makes while eating that they don't want anyone else around at mealtime. That's okay.

Because of the mess, some people feed toddlers before the rest of the family eats. This is undoubtedly better than scolding the child throughout dinner for his absolutely normal messiness.

If you realize how normal this messiness is, and that it will happen at this age, you can probably handle it without too much frustration.

By now, your child will probably be drinking most of his milk from a cup or small glass. If you fill it only one-fourth full, the inevitable spilling will be less of a disaster. Using a spouted "sippy" cup means less spills — which means less frustration for you and your toddler. You can refill it as often as he wants it. Be sure you encourage him to drink plenty of milk.

Toddler Needs Less Food

Rashad stopped eating so much when he was about a year old. He just wanted bottles, but when he hit 1 1/2, he started eating more.

Willadean

Remember that your toddler's appetite is much less than it was. She's not growing nearly as fast as she did those first twelve months. It is during this stage that many parents decide their toddlers are "terrible eaters." "She just doesn't eat a thing," they say.

Meghan is not a good eater. She practically won't touch anything. All she wants is a glass of milk constantly, and it worries me. I told the doctor about it. She laughed and said, "Oh, I can tell you're going through the fun stage."

"What can I do about it?" I asked. She said to give Meghan vitamins with iron, and that seemed to help her appetite. She also told me to quit fussing about it.

I try to avoid candy because I don't like to give them too many sweets. Sometimes when Meghan doesn't want to eat, I think it's because she's too busy to bother. She does love pizza.

Louise, 19 - Meghan, 23 months; Mark, 5 months

Don't try to force or even coax her to eat. Offer small servings of nutritious food. Don't offer sweets at all. If she seems to need an in-between-meal snack, make it part of her daily food plan. Carrots, orange juice, graham crackers, milk, and apple are examples of good snack foods that won't pave the way for your lovely child to become a fat adult.

If you overfeed now, remember, she is likely to have a weight problem when she's grown. You don't want your child to spend her life fighting unhealthy, unattractive fat.

Sean snacks a lot — plums, grapes, nectarines, peaches. He doesn't eat much candy and other sweets. I won't let him. He doesn't need any candy because of his teeth, and because it would spoil his appetite.

Ginger, 18 - Sean, 17 months

It's important she enjoy mealtime.

If she doesn't want to eat any lunch at all, calmly take her food away. She won't starve by suppertime. Just don't tide her over with a handful of cookies an hour later. By mid-afternoon she'll probably be ready for a glass of milk and an apple or other good-for-her snack.

If she eats all her food and asks for more, give it to her in the same way, without an emotional reaction. Whether she eats all her food or not is not what makes her a "good girl."

Serving New Foods

There are a lot of things he won't eat. He doesn't like vegetables. I put them on his plate every night, but if he doesn't eat, I don't force it. My mother is more like, "You have to make him eat," but I don't.

Jessica, 17 - Craig, 2½

Your toddler may appear to like only a few foods. When you offer him a new food, he may refuse even to taste it. Rather than insisting he "clean his plate," serve yourself the same food and show him you like to eat it. Suggest that he might taste it. If he refuses, however, it's okay. There's no need to bribe, force, or push.

Research shows that children who are bribed to eat new foods are less likely to eat that food later than are those who simply are served the food with no bribe involved.

Serve the new food again a few days later. He may be willing to try it, but don't make a fuss if he doesn't. Absolutely nothing is accomplished when mom or dad demands that the child eat the food.

Your child is in control at this point. *You, however, are in control of the foods served.* You don't need to serve soda or other junk foods in your home.

Continue offering her the variety of foods the rest of your family is eating. You may say she won't eat any vegetables at all. What about raw ones? She can get even more vitamins from raw vegetables than from cooked ones.

Until she's two, however, don't give her raw carrot sticks or other hard-to-chew foods because she might choke. You can grate raw carrots for her — she may enjoy stuffing a handful of grated carrots in her mouth — and you'll be happy because you know they're good for her.

Hot dogs may be an all-American food, but they really shouldn't be given to toddlers because of the risk of choking. Even if you slit the skin or slice them into little circles, your child could choke on a piece of hot dog. Besides, hot dogs are high in fat.

Meals and snacks need to be at about the same time every day. Toddlers have small stomachs, and they get hungry within a couple of hours after a meal. If he refuses to eat at mealtime, then asks for a snack immediately afterward, it's generally best not to give it to him. Tell him he must wait until snack time.

Sometimes he may refuse foods he's liked before. This

happened with Lorenzo. Guadalupe and Domingo handled
the situation very well:

> *For awhile Lorenzo wasn't eating very well. He
> didn't like a lot of foods — he was very very picky.
> First it was eggs, then enchiladas, then meat, then
> broccoli. Every time I cooked something, it was, "I
> don't like that."*
>
> *Well, I didn't make him eat it. I would ask why he
> didn't like this because he used to eat it. He would
> just say, "Because I don't like them any more." So I
> wasn't going to make him eat it. I'd ask him if he
> wanted some soup, and he'd say "Yes," and I would
> give him soup.*
>
> *Then one day Domingo got up and made Lorenzo
> some eggs and some meat, and he ate it. We were
> amazed. I guess a little time passed . . . Now he eats
> all those foods again.*
>
> *I know a kid would never appreciate you forcing
> him to eat. He'd withdraw more. I never want to force
> him to do something he doesn't want to do if he
> doesn't really need to do it.*
>
> Guadalupe, 20 - Lorenzo, 4

If Lorenzo's parents had made a big fuss each time he
refused a food, and had insisted that he eat it, he probably
would have become more firmly convinced he didn't like
those foods. Because they didn't let his temporary food
dislikes become a battle between them and their son,
Lorenzo grew out of this food-refusing phase.

Outlaw Junk Food

> *Leah likes grilled cheese sandwiches, macaroni,
> chicken soup. She eats the same stuff we do, and*

*usually she eats pretty well. When she doesn't eat
much, it's usually when she's tired.*

*Every time I go anywhere with anyone, though, it's
"Can Leah have some ice cream?" or "Can Leah
have a cookie?" It's not just that I don't want her to
have this stuff, but I know how she acts — ten minutes
later she's real hyper. If she gets a couple of drinks of
pop, she runs around wild. Usually I give her stuff
without chocolate because it's the caffeine that makes
her crazy.*

Lyra, 18 - Leah, 2 1/2

"Junk food" is food which contains very few nutrients
but is very high in fat, sugar, and calories. You aren't
getting much nutrition at all when you eat junk foods such
as potato chips, French fries, shakes, hot dogs, lunch meats,
cookies, candy, doughnuts, and soft drinks.

Keep the junk food away from your picky eater. If he
isn't hungry enough for meals, he certainly doesn't need a
soda, potato chips, or even cookies an hour later. While one
or two oatmeal cookies provide a little nutrition, a handful
of sugary snacks won't do much for him except ruin his
appetite for more nutritious foods.

If you're in your own home, or if the people you live
with are willing, don't keep junk food there at all. If you
don't have candy and cookies in the cupboard or soft drinks
in the refrigerator, your toddler can't have them while he's
at home. The occasional sweet he gets from the outside
world won't matter that much as long as you aren't
providing them, too.

*She has always eaten good. I let her munch if she
wants to — whole wheat and peanut butter crackers,
but no junk at all. I used to have problems with my
teeth, and I don't want her to.*

> *I think junk food is so bad for you. I used to always*
> *eat stuff like that. No cokes. My doctor said if you*
> *pour coke on a car, it will eat the paint right off!*
>
> Ione, 18 - Lori, 14 months

Fat-Proofing Your Toddler

If you have a toddler who already appears overweight,
don't put him on a reducing diet. Do, however, guide his
eating so that he gains weight more slowly. Make a list of
the food he eats in a three-day period. You may be sur-
prised at the amount of high-calorie food he consumes.

Don't cut out the meat, vegetables, milk, fruit, and
cereal, his basic foods. Do get serious about not having
junk food in the house. If he drinks more than a quart of
milk a day, try diluting it with water. Most doctors don't
recommend skim or low-fat milk for children under two.

Encourage your overweight toddler to get more exercise.
Do you take walks, but push him in his stroller? Get him to
walk with you. Is he outdoors enough? It may take extra
energy on your part to get him to a park if you don't have a
yard, but it may well be worth the effort.

Both Dawn and her daughter, Mercedes, 3, are quite
overweight. Dawn's food habits probably explain both her
own and her daughter's weight problem. Like all children,
Mercedes mimics her mother. She, too, eats a lot of junk
food, then is "picky," as her mother says, at mealtime.

> *I'm a big junk food eater, a nervous eater, and I*
> *pick all the time. A lot of foods you're supposed to*
> *have I don't even like. I like my bacon, fried potatoes,*
> *toast and butter, the eggs — but they have to be done*
> *in grease. For lunch I seldom just make sandwiches*
> *for us. It's McDonald's. If we don't eat breakfast we*
> *usually go to McDonald's, and then have something*

here. We do hit the ice cream man.

Mercedes doesn't eat enough to do anything. In the morning she'll have a bowl of cereal or a couple of pieces of bacon. She doesn't like eggs and doesn't care much for potatoes.

At lunch if we go to McDonald's she'll eat half of a half of a hamburger, plus a half bag of fries, maybe half of her drink. With dinner she will eat at the most ten tiny squares of meat.

Dawn Ellen, 19 - Mercedes, 3

Even at McDonalds, Dawn Ellen's cost for food is fairly high, but she isn't getting much for her money. Mercedes is growing and developing at a rapid rate, and desperately needs better nutrition. Fruits and vegetables should be a

He likes to do it himself.

large part of Mercedes' diet. Yet they're completely missing except for French fries. Neither is she getting any milk.

It's hard for most of us to change our eating habits. That's the big reason so many adults are overweight — but if Dawn Ellen is willing, that's the best way to help Mercedes. She could cut out the trips to McDonalds, forget about the bacon and grease, and start offering Mercedes more nutritious, but still tasty foods.

Mark and Kelly Ellen were eating a lot of junk food. When they realized that Dustin was copying their poor food habits, they decided to change their ways. Mark explained:

For three or four months Dustin had cola all the time. He'd go through all the sodas. The same with Twinkies and cakes. We were drinking a lot of cola and had potato chips everywhere.

Then we realized all that junk food was getting expensive and we were both gaining weight, so we started a little diet. Now we don't even buy sodas. Now we're real conscious about what we eat, and the same goes for him.

For the last year or so, we won't give him junk food. We learned from experience. If he has candy all day, he gets higher and crankier.

Junk food is like a lot of other things. If it's there and it's annoying, just take it away. As you take it away, explain why he can't have it. If we had a box full of cakes and cookies, he'd be into it. So we stopped having junk in the house.

Mark, 22 - Dustin, 21/2

If you want the best for your child, you might decide to follow Mark's example. This would be hard for most of us, but providing good food for your child is a real gift to him.

Nutrition and Extended Family Living

A surprising number of young parents talked about their concern because grandma thinks the baby should have candy and other foods his mother doesn't believe are good for him.

Janis doesn't like to eat a whole lot, or even at all sometimes. So my mom will resort to sweet cereal so she'll eat. I know if you wait until she's hungry, she'll eat what we have.

They give her ice cream and candy, and she'll get cavities too soon. My mom says, "She needs something in her stomach," but all it is is sugar.

Darla, 17 - Janis, 2

Shelly doesn't snack a lot except when she sees somebody eating something. She has very little candy. First of all, she makes a mess, and besides, I don't want her to get cavities. I don't give her soft drinks either, just orange juice or apple juice.

Everybody tells me, "You're so mean, you don't give her any candy. When she gets older, she's going to see all that candy and eat it all."

Even my mother tells me I'm so mean. She makes herself sound like she knows more than I do. She used to always give candy to Shelly behind my back.

One time they were eating chocolates, and I told Shelly she couldn't have any. Then she walked by me, and she had chocolate all over her mouth. It makes me feel bad.

I feel like telling them to mind their own business, but I can't do that. Mom's beginning to do more of that, and it's getting to me. It's building up, and I know I'll wind up telling her something I shouldn't.

Dixie, 18 - Shelly, 17 months

If this is happening in your home, perhaps you could try talking with your family. Could you work out a change? If your family doesn't know much about nutrition, perhaps you could tactfully provide some help on the subject of feeding toddlers. There are lots of well-written and brief pamphlets as well as whole books on this topic.

Do you eat a lot of junk food? If you set a good example for your child by eating mostly nutritious foods, your family may be more likely to respect your wishes concerning your child's nutrition.

If you aren't already doing much of the food preparation, could you offer to help more with the understanding that your child is not to be given junk food?

Of course, you know your family, and you can probably come up with better ideas for changing the situation.

It's Your Responsibility

You have three basic responsibilities here:

- You need to offer him the nutritious food he needs.
- Help him learn that mealtime is a pleasant, sociable time. It's not a period of coaxing him to eat, or a time to argue with the rest of the family.
- Help him stay at a healthy weight.

Your modeling is all-important in the development of your toddler's food habits. If you're a picky eater, or if you survive mostly on junk food, you can expect your child to do the same thing. If you're careful to eat foods from the basic food groups at each meal, your child is more likely to eat well, too.

When this happens, payoff is high in terms of your toddler's health and general development. Her disposition is likely to be better, too, because she'll feel better if she eats the foods she needs.

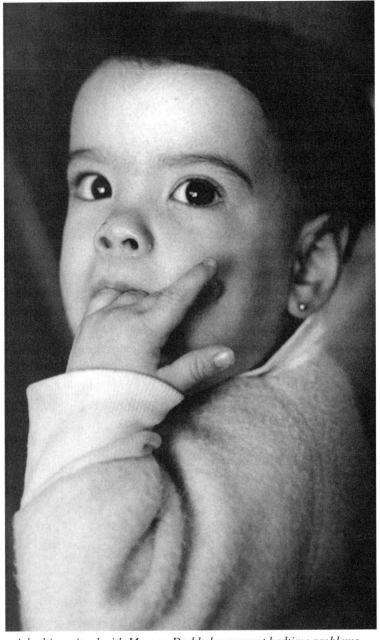

A bedtime ritual with Mom or Dad helps prevent bedtime problems.

7

Importance
of Sleep

Rashad gets tired about 9:30. He has to lie down with my grandpa when he goes to bed. Grandpa sings him a little song and rubs his back and he goes to sleep. He's real attached to Grandpa.

If his grandpa isn't here, he'll lie down next to me. When he goes to sleep, we always put him in his crib.

Willadean, 17- Rashad, 21 months

Luciann still has her pacifier. She goes to sleep with it. The doctor said to slowly take it away, so we only give it to her when she sleeps.

Kiliana, 17 - Luciann, 22 months

Sleep/Rest Important for Toddlers

Your toddler will be less cranky if she eats and sleeps, or at least rests, at regular times. You also need time for yourself. Her daytime naps help both of you.

Most toddlers continue taking a fairly long afternoon nap. Some, however, may not want to nap. It's best to put her to bed anyway, together with her favorite stuffed toy and some books. If she doesn't go to sleep, an hour of quiet play will refresh her for the rest of the day.

Most toddlers do *not* go to sleep willingly. They fill their days with activities, and are very tired by evening. Yet they fight going to bed, especially if others in the family stay up later. In fact, the more tired they get, the more difficulty they may have falling asleep.

Sometimes at around a year, a baby who was fairly easy to get to sleep may suddenly start having a difficult time. He may resist everything about getting ready for bed. At this age, he enjoys being with his parents, and he doesn't want to leave them. He doesn't want to be alone.

When toddlers hit the "I'll do it myself" stage, complete with lots of "No," bedtime may once again become a problem.

Bedtime is a hassle. Henry won't go to bed before I do, and he won't go in his crib. For the last couple of months, he has been in bed with me. If I put him in his crib, he cries and climbs out of it. He goes to sleep with me, then I put him in his crib.

He has his bath after he eats dinner. I put his pajamas on him and get him ready for bed. Then he wants to go outside, and he gets all dirty again.

He goes to bed when we do, but at 6:30 in the morning he doesn't want to get up. Today I brought him to school asleep. I couldn't wake him up.

He used to go to bed earlier. I think the change was when he quit taking a bottle and started playing outside more.

Olivia, 20 - Henry, 23 months

Henry is like most toddlers. He's so busy playing and learning about his world that he doesn't want to take time to sleep. His parents should decide on the time they feel he should be in bed, then see that he gets there at that time.

Getting Henry ready for bed, then allowing him to go outside to play doesn't help him settle down to sleep. If they bathe him a little later and develop a more elaborate bedtime routine with him, he may fall asleep more easily.

Henry would probably be more ready to get up and go to preschool if he went to bed earlier. Perhaps Olivia could gradually change his going-to-bed time to an earlier hour, rather than letting him stay up until his parents go to bed. A bedtime ritual that he enjoys would help.

Importance of Bedtime Ritual

Before he goes to bed, Dalton watches one of those animal videos for about thirty minutes. Then we play with him for thirty minutes, we brush his teeth, and we read several books to him. Sometimes he likes to have his head or his back or his stomach rubbed.

I work three or four nights a week, so if I'm not home, Dalton's dad goes through all this with him. It works pretty well.

Claire, 17 - Dalton, 33 months

Parents often start a bedtime routine when their child is six or eight months old. They find it helps their child settle down to sleep without a lot of fussing. If this isn't working as well now, the solution may be an even more complicated bedtime ritual.

Quiet play, a little snack, a relaxing bath, and looking at a book, with perhaps a lullaby or two, might be a part of your child's ritual for falling asleep. Turning on a night light or some soft music may help, too. One little girl had a certain corner of her blanket which she rubbed on her cheek while she sucked her thumb. To her parent's amazement, she could find that one corner even in the dark. Lots of toddlers need that special blanket when they go to bed:

Derek sometimes drives me up the wall when he won't go to sleep. He has this one blanket that he has to have to go to bed. He's had it all his life. Everybody calls him Linus.

I'll say, "Where's your blanket?" and he'll go get it.

Laurette, 17 - Derek, 18 months

Six months ago, perhaps you read to her, rocked her a few minutes, and put her to bed with her teddy bear. Now she has to have a drink before she kisses you, not after. She may want the same story every night. Perhaps she has to tell each toy "Night-night." Whatever her routine, woe to you if you upset it!

This ritual, if she feels she's in charge, can be a good compromise. You get what you want when she goes to bed without a huge fuss. You each give up something, too. You take the time to go through the ritual with her, and she goes to bed. So don't try to get out of that bedtime story once in awhile just because you're tired. It's important to her.

Juanito has slept through the entire night since he was three months old. He likes to have a glass of chocolate milk before he goes to bed, a bedtime story, and then to bed by 9:30.

Sometimes it's hard because I want to watch TV, but he won't go to sleep if I do. So I turn off the TV

Her favorite doll helps her settle down to sleep.

and make everything dark for thirty minutes, and he goes to sleep.

Kashira, 19 - Juanito, 4

Solving Bedtime Problems

If your child already has a problem going to bed, the solution may not be easy. One young mother, whose husband recently joined the Navy, moved in with her parents-in-law for two months. She then decided she and her daughter would be better off in their own home. But Esperanza's child didn't adapt to coming back home as well as she had hoped:

Juanita is a crybaby. She is really spoiled because I've been at Ruben's mother's house. She got a lot of attention there. When I came back home, I couldn't give her that much attention because I have to do a lot of things here. She won't stay in her crib to take a

*nap. She just screams. I either take her out and set her
in the living room, or I leave her and she screams.*

*She used to sleep three or four hours each after-
noon. Over there she would sleep only 45 minutes or
so. Before, she was always happy, but now she isn't.
She has changed, and I don't understand why.*

*When Juanita was four months old, I got real
attached to her because Ruben was gone. I always
had her by me, and I spent my whole time with her.*

*She hates that crib now, but I hate to put her on my
bed. She sleeps with me a lot. When Ruben comes
home, I guess I'll have to let her sleep with us.*

I should get her used to the crib and let her cry.
                              Esperanza, 17 - Juanita, 12 months

Juanita has had more change than she likes in her first
year of living. First, daddy was home. Then he left. Then
Juanita and mother moved in with a family consisting of
grandma, grandpa, and several young aunts and uncles.
Now she's back in the apartment with her mother and her
other grandma who is gone most of the time.

She's not sure what's going on in her world. First, she
needs a terrific amount of love from mother. But mother is
lonely and unhappy because daddy is gone. It's a difficult
situation any way you look at it.

If Esperanza really wants Juanita to sleep in her crib,
perhaps she should insist, and insist over and over again,
that Juanita sleep there. At the same time, Esperanza needs
to spend much more time with Juanita and try extra hard to
help her feel secure again.

She Doesn't Want to Be Alone

If a baby cries when she's put to bed, it's probably
because she doesn't want to be there. She doesn't want to

be there because she doesn't want to be alone. She would far rather stay out in the living room with her parents. She may feel a bit deserted when she's in bed by herself and mom or dad has firmly shut the door.

One "solution" often tried when baby cries is to get her up again, hoping that in time she will quiet down enough to go to sleep. With this method, she gets to be up with you. She learns that if she cries, she can get up. Why should she go to bed tomorrow night without fussing?

The opposite "solution" is to shut the door even more firmly and leave her alone to cry. A few minutes of crying won't hurt her. If she's tired enough, she'll go to sleep, exactly what you want.

Some toddlers, however, will cry and cry for a couple of hours if left alone. They may fall asleep from exhaustion, but they're not likely to sleep well after such an ordeal. This is the kind of crying Esperanza described. Her solution was to let Juanita sleep with her on her bed. But that wasn't the solution Esperanza wanted.

Every-Five-Minutes Routine

A sensible approach, if your child is at least ten months old, could be a combination of the first two methods. When she cries, go in to see her. Tell her "Good night," pat her back a minute, then walk out. If she continues crying, repeat the process five minutes later. Continue going back in to reassure her every five minutes until she goes to sleep.

She may cry for another hour, but she knows you haven't left her because she's seen you every five minutes. She also knows she won't be brought back into the living room after bedtime.

This method, according to Penelope Leach, author of *Your Baby and Child from Birth to Age Five* (1997: Alfred A. Knopf), will almost always work. Within a week at the most, your toddler should be much more accepting of her bedtime.

Why make such a fuss? Why not let him stay up until he decides he's ready to go to bed? As mentioned before, most toddlers become utterly exhausted before they will give in to sleep. A tired toddler is often a miserable toddler.

A young mother in our school's parenting class described the problem she was having in getting her 14-month-old son to go to bed and to sleep at night. He would get up again and again. He wouldn't go to sleep until very late. In desperation, she often allowed him to stay up far longer than was good for him or for his parents.

I suggested she try the go-in-every-five-minutes-and-pat-his-back routine as a possible solution.

Two days later Jamie returned to report that the every-five-minutes routine had worked. She added, "I was so

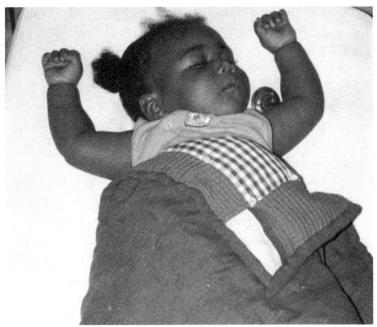

Getting enough sleep is important for both you and your child.

exhausted after those first two nights I couldn't get up to come to school!" The third night, she said, Austin was asleep twenty minutes after she put him to bed.

Night Waking

Lorenzo sleeps very well, but every once in awhile he used to wake up with a nightmare. He'd say he's getting chased by monsters. I would hear him crying, and I'd get up and try to wake him up enough to get him out of his dream.

Guadalupe, 20 - Lorenzo, 4

Your toddler may have a nightmare occasionally. After he's asleep, you hear him screaming. When you go in, he may be kicking or moving frantically. He needs you to reassure him that you're there, that it was only a bad dream.

Go in and talk to him for a minute. Perhaps he would like a drink of water. When he calms down and isn't afraid anymore, tell him "Good night" and go back to bed.

Occasionally young mothers spoke of giving their year-old children several bottles during the night. If he has a bottle at bedtime, he doesn't need the extra food. Again, remember the danger of tooth decay if your child sleeps with a bottle of milk.

If he wakes, instead of handing him a bottle, offer him a cup of water or give him a bottle of water or a pacifier. Tell him "Good night" and walk away. If he continues crying, try the every-five-minutes routine for a week. You'll be exhausted, but if he starts sleeping through the night, think how much better you'll feel the next week.

Because she lived in an apartment, Mariaeliza worried about disturbing her neighbors:

He wakes up at 1 a.m. and wants to watch TV or play with me. If I don't put a movie on, he'll cry and

*scream, and we're upstairs in an apartment. So I play
with him for a little while. A few times I've let him
watch a movie because I'm so tired. It's hard to let
him cry when other people are around.*

Mariaeliza, 17 - Vincent, 3

Perhaps Mariaeliza could talk with her neighbors. If she
wants to try the every-five-minutes routine when Vincent
wakes up, could they cope with his crying for a few nights?
It's worth trying.

Should Child Sleep with Parent?

*Donovan has always slept in his crib in his own
room. But now he's starting to cry and cry when he
goes to bed. I lie down with him for awhile, but lately
he wants to sleep with me. I want him to learn he has
a bed, and that's where he sleeps.*

Belia, 17 - Donovan, 2

"Should" you sleep with your child? Most child development experts in our culture say "No." Some people, however, believe otherwise. Some parents feel it's easier to
sleep with their toddler. Perhaps they just like having the
child sleep in bed with them. As long as everyone is able to
sleep well, it doesn't seem to matter.

However, there may be some problems. One parent or
the other may not be able to get enough rest. Then, of
course, there is the issue of privacy. Children should not
observe lovemaking.

Also, once this pattern has become established, it may be
very difficult to stop. Having their child sleep with them
was described as a problem by several of the young parents
interviewed.

*One thing I did that I wish I hadn't was letting
Heidi sleep with me. When she was little, a newborn, I*

took her to bed with me. She didn't like her crib very much. She would sleep with me all night, and my mom would say, "You have to put her in that crib or she won't ever sleep in it."

She was right. At about five months, I put her in her crib and let her sleep by herself. She didn't like that at all, but after a couple of weeks she was okay. Dennis feels pretty strong about not wanting Heidi to sleep with us.

I have a suggestion for mothers of newborns. If they breastfeed and have the child in bed with them, they should, after they feed him, put him in his own bed.

Jenny, 18 - Heidi, 13 months

Crowded Home Affects Sleeping Habits

Sometimes the fact that the house is more crowded because of the baby creates extra problems. Grandma may want the same rules followed that she remembers using when her children were little. If the baby must share a room with other family members, things get complicated:

My mom doesn't bug me, but she's making me feel like I don't know what I'm doing, like I'm a little kid. For example, Shelly never got used to the crib.

She's in a room with my cousin, and they keep coming in and out, turning on the light, and waking her. So I pick her up and take her in where I sleep, but my mom says I'll have problems later on.

I tell her I can't help it, that I have to get some sleep so I can go to school. She'll sleep there for about two hours, but not the whole night.

If Shelly had the room by herself, I would let her alone.

Dixie, 18 - Shelly, 17 months

Dixie appears to have worked out a rather good solution. Perhaps she needs to share with her mom her reasons for moving Shelly into her room. She might even consider moving Shelly's crib into her room.

It's nice if parent and child can have separate rooms, but often this isn't possible. Shelly might be able to go to sleep more easily if she is routinely put in her crib in Dixie's room. Expecting a toddler to sleep while other children go in and out of the room is expecting a lot.

Sometimes a mother feels she has no choice but to sleep with her baby. There's no room otherwise.

> *Gary wakes up about three times each night. I give him a bottle and change him. He sleeps with me.*
>
> *I had no choice. I didn't want him to, but we moved here when he was about 11/2 months old, and there was no place for the crib. I had to store it away, so he slept with me. Then a month ago my sister moved out, and there was room for the crib. I put it up the other day, but he won't sleep in it.*
>
> *He is really attached to me at night. He won't go to sleep until I do. I hope he outgrows it.*
>
> Jan, 15 - Gary, 12 months

Although Gary has already formed a strong habit of sleeping with his mother, Jan has three choices. She can continue letting him sleep with her. Perhaps he will eventually outgrow it, as she hopes. The danger here is that his mother may suddenly decide at a later time that she doesn't want him in bed with her. It may be even harder to get him to sleep elsewhere then.

She can let him go to sleep in her bed, then move him to his crib. If she chooses this method, she should tell him what she will be doing. She might say, "You may go to sleep in my bed. After you're asleep, I'll move you into your own bed where you will sleep the rest of the night."

Another solution is to insist he sleep in his crib now. Jan could follow the check-on-him-every-five-minutes routine described previously. It will be difficult both for her and for Gary, but it might be worth the effort.

Brigette found a fairly simple solution to a similar problem:

> *Rudy has slept with me at least three-fourths of his life. It got to the point where he wouldn't go to sleep until I was in bed with him. I would lie down with him for about an hour until he was asleep. I strongly recommend you not sleep with your kids — except when they're sick, of course.*
>
> *Now I'll be marrying John, and I don't want Rudy to think John is kicking him out of my bed. A friend suggested I get him a new bed and make a big deal of it. She said I should do this long before my wedding. Then when I get married, it will all be done.*
>
> *I bought Rudy a youth bed. He was thrilled, and it worked. He goes to sleep by himself in his own bed now.*
>
> Brigette, 22 - Joy, 4; Rudy, 3

Remember — Routine Helps

Helping her learn to eat and sleep at regular hours is almost certain to improve your child's disposition. In fact, the "spoiled" toddler who whines a lot and is generally demanding may improve a great deal if she is put on a reasonable time schedule.

With careful planning and your willingness to develop a bedtime routine for your child and to stick to that routine every night, bedtime can be a pleasant experience for you and your child. It can be a time of special closeness between you, a time you both may cherish.

She enjoys books — with you and by herself.

8

Your Amazing Two-Year-Old

Johnnie's not a little baby any-more — he's his own little self. He has his own personality. He doesn't like me to do things for him now, and he's more demand-ing. If he wants it, he wants it now.

I was waiting for him to talk, and now he won't stop. He wants to know about a lot of things.

You know how when they're little, they want you to carry them. Now he doesn't want me to grab him. Now he wants to walk. Sometimes I feel sad because he doesn't want me to do a lot of things.

He mimics me a lot. When I do

my homework, he wants his pencil and his book, and he sits down with me. I'm also watching my language now. If I use a bad word, he's sure to repeat it.

Natalie, 17 - Johnnie, 26 months

New World of Learning

A whole new world opens up to your toddler between her second and third birthdays. She not only has learned to walk and run, but is mastering other skills. She can jump, and she can ride a variety of wheel toys. She is beginning to dress and undress herself. She feeds herself with a little help, and she plays with toys in a much more complex manner. She is fond of crayons and painting.

She loves to imitate the activities of both adults and other children. She will imitate both the way you do want her to behave, and the way you don't want her to behave.

Kalani helps my mom when she's outside cleaning. She gets a broom and tries to sweep with her. When Laramie makes a big mess, she tries to stop him.

Lynnsey, 19 - Laramie, 1; Kalani, 2

She can talk, and is learning new words rapidly. She understands most of what is said to her if it is spoken in simple terms, but she won't always interpret it correctly. Her experience with language is limited. She may appear defiant because she doesn't understand what you want.

Your Child's First Teacher

I read to Leah a lot. She opens the book and reads to herself, too, and she talks to her baby dolls.

Leah talks like a three- or four-year-old, real well. I think it's because we talk to her and read to her that she talks so well. She didn't just wake up one day and start talking like that.

Lyra, 18 - Leah, 2½

Do you plan to be a teacher? Whether your answer is yes or no, you're one already. You are your child's first and certainly most important teacher. If he has been in an infant center or is attending preschool, you have help with your teaching job. You still probably have your child with you during a greater part of his day than do his other teachers. You mean more to your child than any other teacher, too.

> *She's real bright. She's always wanting to learn and know things. She's always asking "Why?" I try to explain to her so she can understand.*
>
> *She watches everything I do now, and she copies me. I brush my hair, and she wants to brush hers. She wants to brush her teeth when I do mine.*
>
> Shalimar, 19 - Ellie, 2 1/2

As he explores, talk with him. Comment on the things around him. When you go for a walk with him, give him a bag to collect treasures — a little rock, a feather, a dandelion. When you return home, talk with him about these items. Now you can also begin to talk about what happened yesterday and your plans for tomorrow because he's beginning to understand the idea of time.

Read to Him Again and Again

> *At night they pick out the books they want to read, and I read to them. Shawna kind of knows what the story is because she almost always picks out the same books every night. Her favorites are the Dr. Seuss books. Before I turn the light off, she wants to look at the book herself.*
>
> *Ever since she was little, before she could even talk, I've taken her to the library when they have the reading programs. I started when she was six months old.*
>
> *Ahmud gets jealous when he sees me reading, so now*

Reading is an important part of their bedtime ritual.

*he sits down and listens, too. Sometimes he gets bored
and goes off and looks at his own book. Then he'll come
back and want me to read.*

Mary, 21 - Shawna, 4; Ahmud, 20 months

Reading regularly, again and again, to your child is
important for his and your enjoyment. It's also an important
part of helping his brain develop well.

Whether or not you have books at home for your child,
visit your public library together. Find out about the
library's storytime for toddlers. Some libraries even have
storytime for infants.

Help your toddler learn early that libaries are great
places. That's where he can check out books that, first,
you'll read to him. When he's older, he'll be reading
to you.

Mary explained why she reads to Shawna and Ahmud
every night whether or not she feels like it:

> *Sometimes when I'm tired, I'd just as soon not
> read, but I don't want them to think if you're tired
> you don't read. So we read anyway. When they're
> in school they can't quit reading just because
> they're tired.*
>
> Mary

Developing language skills is perhaps your child's most
important task this year. You help her each time you talk
with her, sing to her, tell her stories, and read to her. You
also help her when you listen to her. Encourage her to tell
you stories. Ask her to tell you about the book you've been
reading to her every night for the past month. You may find
she has it memorized! Of course you don't expect her to
actually read for several years yet.

Watching and listening to your child as she develops
speaking ability is exciting. Remember the baby who could
only communicate with you by crying? She's come a
long way!

"I Love You, Mommy"

You probably are thrilled when your toddler says "I love
you." All parents like those words. Toddlers, however, are
emotional little people whose feelings change quickly. The
"I love you, Mommy" may turn into "I hate you" ten
minutes later because you couldn't allow him to do
something he wanted to do. You probably will feel hurt or
angry the first time this happens.

> *Mickey says "No" and tells me I'm not his friend
> any more. I tell him I'm his friend and I still love him.*
>
> *He will say "No, you're not my friend," and walk
> away. A few minutes later he comes back and decides
> we're friends.*
>
> Susan, 20 - Mickey, 2 1/2; Felicia, 11 months

Instead of showing your anger, reassure him that you love him a lot and you're sorry he's feeling that way right now. Of course you won't let him kick or hurt you when he's angry — or any other time. Give him a chance to talk about his feelings if he wants to. Your patience and calm reaction will help him deal with his anger.

To Bed, to Sleep?

Fatigue is another factor that influences behavior. Toddlers are very active and tire quickly. Many resist napping. Simple fatigue and disruption of her normal sleeping schedule is at the root of many behavior problems. Recognizing this and adjusting expectations may make life easier for everyone.

If your child doesn't go right to sleep when she goes to bed, it doesn't necessarily mean she doesn't need to rest. Most two-year-olds will be better off if they continue their afternoon naps.

If she doesn't want to go to sleep, tell her that it's all right. She can play quietly in her bed. Give her some books and a quiet toy. Ask her to play there for an hour. She might like a timer set so she can get up when it dings. Chances are she'll go to sleep. If she doesn't, she will still get the rest she needs.

You'll also appreciate the quiet time. Perhaps you can nap at the same time. If you're feeling impatient with your child, a nap for each of you may be the best approach.

No Mealtime Arguments

We all like mealtime to be pleasant. Mealtime arguments can spoil everyone's appetite. Now is the time, while your child is small, to start the habit of happy mealtimes. Fussing at your child to get him to eat will get you nowhere.

Most toddlers gain only three to five pounds between 12

and 24 months, and another three to five pounds by age 3. It's important for you to understand this slower growth rate because this means your toddler may not need to eat as much as you think he should.

Toddlers may go through stages when they will eat only a few foods. It's okay to have a limited diet as long as it's balanced. Try to have something from each of the food groups each day (milk, protein foods, fruits, vegetables, bread group). His diet may seem monotonous to you, but that's all right.

Children who are served nutritious food and very little junk food tend to eat when they're hungry. If they aren't hungry, they probably shouldn't eat anyway. So don't nag! Instead, use mealtime to talk about what's happening today.

If it's just you and your child, you can talk about the shape and color of the food, how it was prepared, where milk comes from, and other topics of interest to your child. If other family members are present, conversation won't be so child-centered, but it can still be concerned mostly with the pleasant happenings of the day.

"Where Do Babies Come From?"

Your toddler may start asking questions about sex. If he does, let him know you appreciate his questions, then answer in terms he can understand. When he asks, "Where do babies come from?" you might say, " Babies grow in a special place in the mother's body."

If he asks how the baby got inside the mother, you can tell him that a mother and a father make a baby together. You might explain that the father's sperm gets into the mother through the father's penis.

Sometimes little girls worry because they have no penis, and little boys worry that their penis might come off. Explain that boys and girls are made differently. Teach

your child the correct names for his/her genitals. Name
them as you name other body parts.

All little boys and girls handle their genitals. When they
do, and find that this feels good, they may masturbate. This
does no harm. It is normal, and you would be wise to
ignore it. A parent who tells his/her child that masturbation
is bad may cause the child to feel naughty, or to think that
sex or sexual feelings are bad. That's not a very realistic or
healthy approach.

Potty Training (Teaching)

*He's 30 months old now. Toilet training is one
thing that's very difficult right now. He loves wearing
training pants, and he says he's a big boy then.*

*He knows why he has to go in the toilet, but he's
scared when he has to do #2. For about two days he
went pretty good. He'd try so hard, but sometimes
he'd start crying. I'd leave him there, and he'd come
running and pee on the carpet.*

*Sometimes he goes into the bathroom, and he will
say, "Take my diapers down." He will pee with his
dad, but he's not ready for #2. Sometimes on the
weekends I let him wear his underwear, and he will
tell everybody. But if he has to go pee, he will wet
his pants.*

Jessica, 17 - Craig, 2½

This little boy is showing many signs of stress, and his
parents are, too. He wants to succeed and please his
parents, but developmentally he's not quite ready. It would
be better to wait a month or two, then try teaching again.
By then he may have developed the ability to hold his urine
or release it when he chooses. He may be more able to
control his bowel movement (BM), too.

Little boys often learn later than little girls. Many are unable to learn until they're three or even older. It's a lot less stressful and more productive not to try teaching him to go to the toilet until he's developmentally ready.

We're trying to potty train her. There's not really a hurry, but I want her to understand. I'll say. "Mom has to pee pee," and she'll take me to the bathroom. She knows when to flush. Sometimes she goes on the potty and we all cheer for her.

Liliana, 17 - Luciann, 22 months

Often a child will like to use the potty at first. He may enjoy the new training pants or potty chair, but the added attention he's getting is probably more important to him. He may lose interest as toileting settles into a routine. Putting him back in diapers, and trying again a month or so later is a good idea.

If you can be relaxed about toilet teaching, it will be much easier for everyone. For a broader discussion of this topic, see *Discipline from Birth to Three* by Lindsay and McCullough.

Hard to Accept Change

The last couple of days Ellie wants me all the time. She wants to be with me 24 hours a day. Her father left two months ago, and she's happier now, but I think that made her feel a little insecure.

Shalimar

Ellie may be " happier now" that her father is gone, but at the same time, she undoubtedly misses him. She needs some extra attention from her mother for awhile. For all kinds of reasons, your child may become more dependent on you at about age two, especially if you have to be separated from him for awhile. It's hard for children of this

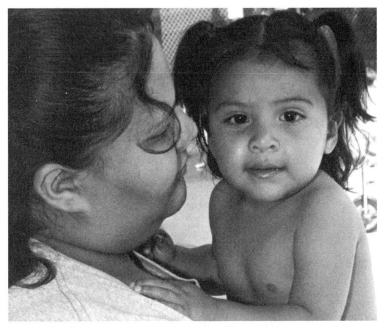

Big changes are hard for toddlers. She needs her mommie.

age to cope with change in their lives. If you must leave your child with a new babysitter, let him have time to adjust to the person before you leave. A big change like dad leaving or even the family moving into a different home may be especially difficult for your toddler.

If you're moving, prepare in advance. Talk to your child about it. As you pack, let him pack some of his toys in a box. You may need to repack them later, but if you let him be a part of the process, it will all seem less strange to him.

Tell him how the furniture and clothing, and especially his toys, will be moved from one place to the other. Explain what your new home will be like, and where he will sleep and play. Let him see it in advance if possible. The more familiar the moving process is to him, the less anxious he is likely to be.

Toddlers are more secure when their life has a predictable routine. They want to sleep in their own bed with a special blanket or stuffed animal. Mom or dad may be the only ones who can put them to bed without tears. The same may be true of eating. They want a predictable routine.

Even More Patience Needed

While your two-year-old may appear clingy and dependent at times, at other times she will insist on doing things her way:

> *If she sets her mind on something, she'll do it whether I want her to or not. If I want to do her hair, she won't let me do it. She gets in these moods where she won't let anybody touch her. In fact, sometimes she kicks and she screams over almost nothing.*
>
> Shalimar

This can be a difficult time for a toddler. She wants so much to be independent, but simply can't do everything she wants to do. It's best to allow time for her to dress and undress herself, and to be available when she can't quite do it alone. At times she will be cooperative, and at other times, extremely unreasonable. Develop your patience to the fullest. This is not the time to allow yourself the luxury of being impatient. Your toddler needs your help to cope with her moodiness.

> *He doesn't listen to us. He always likes to do his own thing, and he's demanding. He says "No" to everything, and he always asks "Why?"*
>
> Sarah, 17 - Leon, 2 1/2

Now you need to be especially consistent in your interactions with your child. If you tell her one thing today, you need to follow the same rule tomorrow.

Routine is important for two-year-olds. She likes to do

things the same way day after day after day. Her bedtime
routine may become even more elaborate.

These are busy months for you and for your toddler. She
still has much to learn about her world. If she's given
plenty of opportunity to explore, as we've said so often in
these books, she'll learn more. She also will keep you alert
as you supervise her exploring!

> *People say she's spoiled, but I don't let her go too
> far. She's a kid, and they explore and they do things.
> If you put too many limitations on a child, you never
> know how much she can learn.*
>
> Shalimar

Winning — For Both of You

Talking about a power struggle between a grown-up
(you) and your toddler may sound silly. Of course you have
the power if we're talking about physical force. If your
child won't go to bed, you can pick her up, even if she's
kicking and screaming, and put her in her bed.

If you do this, who wins? Certainly not your child. And
you don't win either if she's crying and screaming and
extremely unhappy.

Try to get inside your toddler's head for a minute. How
does she feel? At the same time, think about how you feel.
What can you do so you *both* will win?

Time may be a big factor in this kind of stress. You have
a great deal to do. If you're in school and/or have a job, you
need to get a lot done while you're with your child. It's
normal to try to hurry her at mealtime, when she's getting
dressed, and when it's time for her to go to bed. As she
feels pressured, however, she's likely to dawdle even more.
Perhaps she'll declare flatly that she's not going to eat, or
go to bed, or get dressed, or whatever it is she must do.

Experiment with taking ten more minutes to get her ready for school. Stretch that bedtime routine a little more. You may find she's more likely to go along with what you want her to do.

Setting a timer might help. For example, show her a timer set for ten minutes. Explain that when the timer dings, lunch will be ready. Toddlers tend to be completely absorbed in their play and dislike being interrupted. They need closure. Advance notice that it's almost time to change activities may help her cooperate.

You're His Model

I think it's very very hard being a parent. I don't regret it, but I wish I had waited. Seeing Johnnie grow up as a little person is making me think twice before I act because he mimics me and looks up to me.

I'm the person he copies, his role model. I used to dip cookies in my milk, and Johnnie started doing that. My boyfriend said, " If you don't want your son to do that, you can't do it." He was right, of course.

Natalie

Being your child's role model is an awesome responsibility. Observe your child playing with dolls and you're likely to learn how you sound to him. Children whose parents yell a lot often yell at their dolls. It is also true that children whose parents take the time to explain their activities to their child may find him talking in a similar fashion with his "baby."

Toddlers need a lot of attention. They're growing and learning rapidly. Positive attention from significant persons makes the learning seem more meaningful and important.

Watching him learn is exciting for you. Experiencing that learning is even more exciting for your toddler.

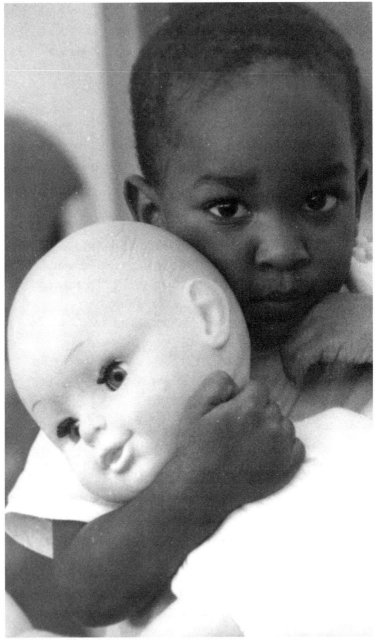

Many two-year-olds enjoy playing with dolls.

9

Playing with Your Two-Year-Old

School is important, but it's not more important than Leah. If Leah says she wants to sit with me or play with me, and that means I won't get all my homework done, I'll do it.

The important thing is to listen to your child and spend time with her. You can't have so much to do that you can't play with her or talk with her. You have to manage your time.

Lyra, 18 - Leah, 2½

Skye plays real good by herself. She puts the rope and the beads together.

She makes believe a lot. She flies children around the room

*and tells me she's flying all over the house. Yesterday
she told me she made a choo-choo train.*

*When I go to softball practice, Skye and her dad
pick me up afterward. She'll say, "Mommy, I play
softball?"*

I say, "Not until you're bigger."

She'll say, "Okay."

*Or she'll say, "I go to school, Mommy, I go to
school?" I tell her not yet. Or when I'm doing my
homework, she puts her colors in her backpack and
tells me she's going to school, and she's doing her
homework.*

*We listen to sing along tapes, and Skye loves to
sing and she likes to dance. Every time a song comes
on that she likes, she'll say, "Mom, let's dance!"*

Molly, 18 - Skye, 33 months

Sometimes She's Self-Sufficient

Your two-year-old is more self-sufficient now. She can
play by herself, but she still loves and needs your attention.
If you play with her regularly, she will learn more. She'll
also be more willing to play by herself other times.

This doesn't mean you need to spend all your time
entertaining her. That wouldn't be good for her either.
Some of the time she'll be satisfied to play near you while
you do your work.

Made-at-Home Toys

Even if he owns a lot of toys, your toddler is likely to
prefer homemade items much of the time. One of the best
toys you can give him is a big box. If you or someone you
know buys a new TV or, even better, a refrigerator or other
big appliance, save the box.

Your toddler will love going in and out of it. Together

you can cut windows and doors in his new house. He can decorate it with crayons or paints. He can pretend it's his home one day, a school house the next. He can hide from you in his house. You'll hear him giggling as you look for him.

Use a smaller box for a cook stove. Turn the box over and help your toddler draw burners on the bottom. Help him "cook" a snack for the two of you, then "eat" with him.

Encourage him in his pretend play. He may have an imaginary friend. He may even talk to his friend. Imaginary play is a healthy part of growing up.

Larissa loves Winnie the Pooh. She has a Pooh Bear, and she puts him in his little crib and tells him "Night-night." She rocks his little crib and pretends like she's putting him to sleep.

She has little fake baby food, and she feeds him. On the weekends she'll pretend like the school bus is outside. She'll go over to her bear and say, "The bus is coming. I have to go now."

Leila, 18 - Larissa, 2½

Do you have a card table you can set up near you? Drape a sheet or blanket over it, and your toddler has a tent or a cave or whatever he wishes. Let his imagination take over.

When you're cleaning out your closets, choose some cast-offs for a dress-up box for your child. He'll like old hats, scarves, mom's or dad's shoes, and other grown-up clothing. Include costume jewelry that's safe for your child, things he can't swallow. Encourage your toddler to pretend he's someone else as he dresses up.

Time for Finger Painting

Let him finger paint. Of course he'll taste and examine the paint first. Then he may paint a little.

Finger painting takes some preparation. Put old clothes on your child and lots of newspapers on the floor. A small chair and table with lots of working space would be ideal, but a high chair will do.

Recipe
You can make a safe (from a tasting standpoint — it still makes a mess!) finger paint by mixing two tablespoons of cornstarch into two tablespoons of cold water. Then add one cup boiling water and stir again.
For color, use food coloring . Or use one tablespoon of yellow prepared mustard to two tablespoons of the base to make a canary yellow paint.

Almost any kind of plain paper is all right for finger painting — brown wrapping paper, paper bags, cardboard from shirt and panty hose packages. Tape the paper to the table or tray before he starts painting. Or you could let him finger paint in the bath tub — with supervision, of course.

After all this preparation, he may do more tasting than painting. Show him how to use the paint on the paper. He may find the whole thing a bit weird, but he'll probably have a ball. He'll enjoy it even more if you paint with him.

Take a tip from preschool teachers and do a little organizing of your child's day. Plan a time when she can finger paint or paint with a brush. If the weather permits, painting outside cuts back on cleanup time. Provide plenty of opportunities for your toddler to color, paint, cut paper (with blunt-ended scissors), and other creative activities. You'll continue to supervise, of course:

In my house the crayons are up in the closet where Mickey can't reach. It's special when he can color, or paint, or cut paper. If he wants to cut 100 pieces of paper, that's fine, but he must do it in a special place.

Susan, 20 - Mickey, 2½; Felicia, 11 months

She's not ready to color or paint between the lines in a coloring book. In fact, if she's at all creative, she won't "be ready" later either. Coloring books are a poor investment. Giving her big pieces of paper, then encouraging her to draw or scribble as she thinks best is a far better approach.

Luke likes to write a lot. I open big paper bags and turn the blank side out. I tape it on the wall, and it's like a big chalkboard. He writes all over it. That keeps him busy for a long time. Of course I have to watch that he stays on the paper.

Ashley, 18 - Luke, 34 months; Abby, 20 months

Don't worry whether your child uses her left or her right hand. Children often appear to change handedness several times before settling into using one or the other as their "working" hand. Whichever hand she uses is okay. The important thing is not to try to change her preference.

By her third birthday, you probably can tell whether she's right or left handed. If she's left handed, she's part of the 15 percent of the population with this preference.

Teaching with Games

You can teach your child colors by talking about the color of his clothes and of other things around him. You can make games by coloring circles of paper various bright colors. Then draw the same size circles on a sheet of paper and color those circles to match the others. Can he match the red cut-out circle with the red circle on the paper?

Does your toddler know his name? If he is separated from you, can he tell someone who he is? You can help him learn by making it a game. Ask him to name family members in photographs, and include photos of him.

Doll play is important to many two-year-olds. If you have another baby now, your toddler may be especially interested in his own baby.

Haley has a friend who comes over a lot. They play in the playhouse with their dolls. They change them and talk to them.

She'll say, "We're going bye-bye. We have to get ready for school," like I do every morning. One time I heard her say, "Oh-h-h, I'll tell grandma on you."

Bettiann, 20 - Haley, 35 months

Helping Mom and Dad

Pretend play for a two-year-old often means imitating mom or dad.

Ricardo wants to do everything I do. When he sees me cooking, he wants to cook. When his dad says he's hungry, Ricardo runs to the kitchen and wants to fix him something. I let him bring the food to his daddy, and he feels great.

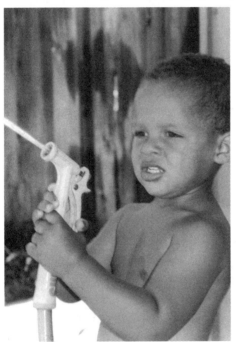

Sometimes when I'm washing the dishes Ricardo wants to help me. I say, "Ricardo, come here and help me," and he comes running in. He brings his chair over to the sink, and I let him rinse the dishes.

Sharon, 19 - Ricardo, 35 months; Monique, 16 months

He's watering the yard.

By the time your child is three years old, he'll be able to

"help" you in many ways. He can set the table, especially if you provide light-weight plastic dishes. He can help make his own snack by putting some grated cheese on a tortilla, folding over the tortilla, and heating it, with your help, either in the microwave or the regular oven. He can help carry in the groceries.

He can dust furniture, although you want to be careful about giving him a treated dust cloth because you don't want him to put it in his mouth. He'd love to "work" with a feather duster. He can help pick up trash. In fact, he may be willing to help you do all sorts of things. For most children of this age, the magic word is *help*. He probably won't be willing to take on all these jobs simply because you ask him to. His incentive in doing jobs is to be like you.

Celebrating Holidays

Donovan saw Santa, and he was scared. We went to the mall, and he didn't like Santa much. That was okay. We didn't have to take a picture. We were in line, and he saw the little kids going to Santa. He said, "No, I don't want it." So we left, and everything was fine.

Belia, 17 - Donovan, 2

You may be eager to share Halloween with your child. Or you may be looking forward to introducing your toddler to Santa Claus at your local department store. You may find, however, that your little one is not thrilled with either experience.

Dalton loves Halloween and Christmas, but Santa, no. He's not too sure of the big fat guy in red.

Claire, 17 - Dalton, 33 months

Santa Claus may scare your toddler because she thinks he's real. He's big and fat, he wears funny clothes, has a peculiar beard, and he sits there and glares at her. She may burst into tears and ruin your photograph.

Halloween scares many toddlers for the same reason. They don't understand fantasy, and they believe these outlandish characters are real.

To help make these events less frightening, talk to your toddler beforehand about where you're going and what you'll see. Maybe you can practice. Show her pictures of Santa. Play with masks together before Halloween.

When the day arrives, don't rush your child into this new experience. Let her watch other children climbing on Santa's lap. Don't pressure her to follow their lead. She may decide it's okay, or she may not. If she doesn't want to see Santa this year, respect her feelings. Perhaps she'll be ready next year.

On Halloween, she might like to hand out candy to the trick or treaters while you hold her.

How Much Television?

People shouldn't use TV as a babysitter. It rots their brain, and they don't have an interest in read- ing. Sergy and Leonardo have a lot of books, and I tell them to read or play with their toys instead of settling for television.

I let them watch two shows, and that's a whole hour. At this age, that's enough. My best friend lets her son watch videos all day. We'd rather go to the park instead.

Kerrianne, 19 - Sergy, 3; Leonardo, 4

In many families, television viewing is a fact of life. The set will be tuned into a variety of programs throughout the day and evening. If you're in your parents' home, you may not have much control over television viewing.

Television probably does more to prevent learning for children under three than it teaches them. This is true even when the programs are carefully selected and limited to those which are supposed to be appropriate for the young child.

Your child needs to interact actively with his environment to learn about it. He needs to smell, taste, feel, and handle objects with his hands to discover what they're like and what he can do with them. Just looking and listening isn't enough.

Unfamiliar objects seen on the screen have little or no meaning. He may not even recognize familiar objects. Yet without guidance, a child may appear to be content in front of the TV screen:

> *Alina will sit in a chair and watch TV for hours if she has her pillow, and she can hold it and suck her thumb.*
>
> Joanne, 23 - Francene, 4; Alina, 3; Gloria, 1

Alina, like all children, needs to run, crawl, jump, roll, and climb. Children enjoy doing these things with other children because they're beginning to learn social skills. These skills need to be actively practiced. That doesn't happen in front of the TV.

Although a child may hear many words spoken on television, watching too much TV is likely to delay her language development. If she's absorbed in the TV, she isn't talking, and learning to talk takes lots of practice. If she does try to speak, no one is there to answer. She needs to talk to someone who will respond to her.

Select Programs Carefully

> *We don't want Elena watching horror films. In fact, I don't think a child should watch that much TV.*

It's not good for their development. There's too much
violence, and it can pollute their minds.

Raul, 19 - Elena, 23 months

When your child watches TV, you need to select her
programs carefully. So much of television has strong
emotional situations which are upsetting to children. It's
not real, it gives a distorted view of violence, a distorted
view of sex, and has enormous emotional overload for
your child.

Luciann seldom watches more than 30 minutes of
TV. I don't want her to watch violent shows because
she picks up things from everywhere. I don't want her
to be more violent.

Liliana, 17 - Luciann, 22 months

Programs showing violent behavior and angry people
may be quite disturbing to her. She may not fully understand what she sees, and her ability to use words is too
limited for her to be able to talk about it.

If other people are interested in watching the program,
they may even tell your child to be quiet. They may discourage the few questions she might have tried to ask.

Any program your child watches should be suitable for
his age, and it should be viewed with someone who will
talk to him about it. Ideally, children under three should not
watch TV for more than an hour each day.

If you live in a home where the television is on regularly
for long hours, try to keep your child away from the set and
its noise. You can rescue the kids — put them in a separate
room with toys away from the TV.

If you watch a lot of TV, your child may follow your
example and miss out on the active play she needs. Or she
may take advantage of your involvement with television
and get into trouble:

When I get stuck on the TV, it's as if they say, "Forget it." They go off and do things I don't let them do. When I don't pay any attention to them, they get into all kinds of things.

Joanne

Even if you enjoy watching TV, you may decide to sacrifice some of your shows to spend time with your child. You're a far better teacher than the television can ever be. Let her have the advantage of your companionship rather than letting the TV set become her companion.

Research shows that aggressive children tend to watch a lot of violence on television. Research also shows that children who watch too much TV show less imagination in their play and at school than do children who watch less television.

A toddler who sits in front of the TV set for several hours each day is not involved in the active play he needs. He's also undoubtedly watching shows inappropriate for him — shows with scary scenes, shows which give a distorted view of relationships between men and women, and other situations which tend to scare or confuse him. Even the evening news often includes frightening coverage of the day's violence.

Children can learn important things from television, however. Can you watch TV with your child and talk with him about what he sees and hears? If the two of you watch an hour of carefully selected shows a day, and talk together about it, TV may have a positive influence on your toddler.

If your family watches a lot of TV, you may have little choice in the number of hours the set is on each day. Probably the best tactic in this case is to find a quiet place where you and your child can play away from TV. Or take him outside to play, and encourage him to run around. He probably prefers games with you over the television.

She's practicing her balancing skills at the park.

Playing Outside

*If it's nice, we play outside, or we go to the park. I
name everything, the leaves and the sky, and talk
about the colors.*
                                                    Molly

Playing outside is important to two-year-olds. If you're
lucky enough to have a fenced-in yard, she'll probably
spend hours there, especially if you can be with her. Remember that she still needs lots of supervision. If your yard
is not securely fenced, you'll need to be with her constantly
when she's outside.

Toddlers love to play in sand, dirt, and mud. Give him
spoons, cups, and other sand toys. It's best to keep a sand-
box covered when he's not playing in it. This keeps out the
cats and dogs who like sand, too.

He can paint the garage or outside wall if you get him a
small bucket of water and a paint brush. He'll love playing
with a squirt bottle filled with water. By now he may be
able to blow soap bubbles.

If you don't have a yard, can you take him to a nearby park often? Taking him for a walk each day will satisfy some of his need to be outside. Of course this won't be the kind of walk where you get lots of exercise from walking rapidly. Your toddler will explore all sorts of things along the way. He'll be in no hurry.

Outings to the airport to watch the planes landing and taking off, to the train station, and to a building site will excite him as much as taking him to Disneyland. Of course, if you're observing a construction site, you and your child will hold hands as you watch.

> *We stop for fire engines. We go to the harbor and watch the boats. Haley points at helicopters going over and says, "Copters."*
>
> *We take her to a petting farm where there are chickens and goats. Haley likes to pet them. We started going there when she was 2.*
>
> *We also go to the park and feed the ducks.*
>
> Bettiann

If you live near a beach, you and your toddler may enjoy playing there. Of course you'll be constantly watching her. You also need to be extra careful about sunburn. Most toddlers have sensitive skin and burn easily.

> *She loves the beach. When the waves go out, she runs down, then runs back when they're coming in. She likes chasing birds, and loves to lie in the sand.*
>
> Shalimar, 19 - Ellie, 2 1/2

What About Cold Weather?

Toddlers enjoy playing outside. It's good for them. They are usually more active outside than inside. The exercise helps their motor development. It also gives them a better appetite and makes them more ready for bedtime.

But what about cold weather? Claire doesn't much like the cold, so Mitch plays in the snow with Dalton:

Dalton and his dad make snowmen, and they have little snowball fights. I'm not big on cold weather, but I usually watch from the window with a cup of hot chocolate.

Claire

On the other hand, Cathi says:

Susie loves to go outside, but it's cold already. She has to be inside a lot or she'll get sick. We try to explain, but she's still too little to understand.

Cathi, 18 - Susie, 34 months

This sounds like a power struggle. Cold temperatures don't make babies sick. Germs do. Usually a preschool child can be bundled up warm enough not to get cold when she's playing outside. Susie is probably quite active while she's playing and may not feel cold at all.

The mother may have a much bigger problem trying to stay warm. Cathi may not be dressed as warmly, and she is undoubtedly less active than her child.

The mother should claim the problem. She should tell her daughter that she's cold and needs to go back in the house now to get warm. Together they could work on some rules for outside play such as the length of time they'll stay outside. It might help if an indoor play area with room for active play could be arranged for days when she really can't go outside.

An Athlete Already?

I think Luke's going to be a good baseball player. His dad likes to play baseball with him. When we play, Luke knows how to hold his little plastic bat real good. He hits the ball a lot when we throw it at him.

Ashley

Lots of fathers and mothers look forward to playing ball with their children. By the time she's two, dad may be playing catch with her. She's not ready for rules yet, but she may thoroughly enjoy playing ball her way with mom or dad.

Leon's parents described his ball-playing mania:

> **Jordan:** *Leon watches basketball with me. He knows how to dribble a basketball already. He doesn't like to play with trucks, but he plays with balls constantly.*
>
> **Sarah:** *When I tell him to throw his clothes in the hamper, he shoots them in, and yells, "Two points!" He watches sports on TV all the time with his dad.*

Rough-housing is an activity that toddlers and parents, especially dads, often enjoy. It's not smart, however, to play at hitting each other if you don't want your child to hit other children. Neither is it wise to get your child so excited that he'll have trouble calming down.

> *I think parents set the pace. My husband likes to play rough. Then he gets tired and wants to stop, but the kids aren't ready to stop. You can't just all of a sudden stop. You have to start going slower and taking it easier. It took him awhile to learn that.*
>
> Annabel, 27 - Andrew, 10; Anthony, 7; Bianca, 5; James, 2

Active play usually is not a good idea at bedtime. You want your child to slow down. That's why a bedtime routine including a storytime works best.

The whole world is fantastic to your toddler. Everything is new. A toddler really doesn't need Disneyland because he can find excitement wherever he is. Your job is to share his excitement, and to guide and support him as he discovers his world. *Have fun!*

He needs to hold your hand when you cross a parking lot.

10

Guarding Your Toddler's Health and Safety

One day I smelled something burning, and I saw smoke coming out of the oven. Vincent had turned it on! That's when I decided to take the control knob off and put it up where he couldn't find it.

Yesterday he broke a glass, and he wanted to pick up the pieces. He likes to help — but of course I took him away and cleaned up the glass myself.

Mariaeliza, 17 - Vincent, 3

Kamie slides the chair over, and gets up on the counter. She's been standing on the top part of the couch, the back of it. Last night she was jumping off the couch.

*She fell off and sprained her ankle, but by today she
was ready to jump off the couch again. I told her,
"No more."*

*I put away the stuff that would be dangerous. I
moved plants up to a higher cabinet she couldn't
reach. I didn't want anything to happen to her.*
Lucas, 21 - Kamie, 21 months

Your Toddler Needs Even More Supervision

*We're in an apartment, and sometimes there's
broken glass on the sidewalk. I pick it up when I see
it, but I can't get it all.*

*Luke and Abby like to go barefoot outside. Once
Luke stepped on some glass and cut his foot, so now
he wears shoes. In hot weather he likes sandals.*
Ashley, 18 - Luke, 34 months; Abby, 20 months

You probably were quite safety conscious during your
child's first year. You didn't leave him alone even for a
minute on a bed or changing table even though you "knew"
he couldn't turn over. You realized how quickly a baby can
roll off such a surface.

When your baby started crawling, you may have
checked out your home at his eye level. This is a good way
to spot the dangers. You probably covered the electric
outlets, and perhaps you were able to child-proof your
home to a great extent.

Your toddler needs even more careful watching than he
did a few months earlier. He's running everywhere, but his
judgment develops much more slowly. During this sensory
motor stage, the steady supervision must continue. He has
to try things to find out what will happen, yet he's unable to
think it through and predict what will really happen. It's
your job to keep him safe.

Don't ever leave your baby or toddler alone in your

house or apartment, even if he's sleeping. Don't ever leave him alone in your parked car either, even if you're just running into the store for one quick item.

Children left in cars in the summer can die from the heat. Closed cars get much hotter than the outside air, somewhat like an oven. There is also the danger the child will lock the doors and not be able to get out in an emergency.

He can probably turn doorknobs and open doors by his second birthday. It's even more important that you keep dangerous things out of his sight and out of his reach. It's doubly important to keep trash cans securely covered or in a closed-off area when toddlers are running around. A small child can get in lots of trouble by playing in the trash.

Check your home again for hazards. Many almost-toddlers climb amazingly well even before they walk. Climbing means she can get into even more trouble if you don't watch her constantly.

> *Nathan doesn't know. The whole world is a big adventure, and that's scary. He could fall on some-thing, and he always wants to put things in his mouth. It takes 24 hours of supervision — unless he's sleeping. Then you can finally relax.*
>
> *My grandpa does a lot of watching because when I was little, I almost died when I choked on an apple. He's there watching, watching, being protective. Nathan is really quick and, when he's outside, he can run out in the street so fast.*
>
> Esteban, 18 - Nathan, 2; Ralph, 5 months

Protect Him from Burns

> *One day I left my curling iron on the bathroom counter. I had turned it off, but it was still hot. Haley went into the bathroom and put her hand on it. She*

started screaming, "I touched hot. I touched hot."
It made a blister, and I put ice on it. The doctor
said not to pop the blister, so I didn't.

> Bettiann, 20 - Haley, 35 months

Toddlers are at great risk for being burned. They can be scalded by pulling a cup of coffee or tea off the table onto themselves. They can be burned by touching a hot stove, iron, or heater. When you're carrying hot food to the table, you must be extremely careful. If your toddler is playing on the floor beside you, you could spill hot food on him.

When he's learning to walk, his ability to reach develops rapidly. The child who was confined to crawling on the floor last week may be pulling himself up by grabbing the table or the stove this week. Hot food, liquids, and heavy items must *not* be left near the edge of the table or stove.

Make sure the things he can climb are safe for him.

Poisoning Is Big Danger

One time I left a cup of bleach up on the sink. I guess Luke thought it was water and he drank it. I smelled something, and I realized the smell came from his mouth. I ran to get my mother. By the time we got back, my husband had put his finger down Luke's throat and made him throw up.

Now we don't leave anything like that lying around. We're also careful about small objects because the kids could choke on them.

Ashley

Children are most likely to be poisoned when they're ten to twenty months old. They move around a lot, explore everything in reach, put everything possible in their mouths, and aren't able to understand what's dangerous and what's not. They also will drink things that taste terrible (to us).

Cigarettes are poisonous. If members of your family smoke, use your best negotiating skills to get them to help keep ash trays out of the reach of your toddler.

The fact that your toddler goes everywhere and explores everything is exciting because you know that's how he's learning. It's also scary because you know how easily he can be hurt. If it's a white powder, he thinks it's sugar. If it's a colored liquid, it must be juice. It may actually be a poisonous perfume or insecticide, but he probably won't know the difference.

It's your job to keep your child safe. Check your house, garage and yard often for items that could be dangerous to touch or eat. Know the plants around your home. Oleander and castor beans, for example, are dangerous if eaten, and can kill a child.

Find the telephone number of your nearest Poison

Control Center. Keep it by your phone along with your doctor's and other emergency numbers. If you think your child has been poisoned, take any evidence you have of what he swallowed, a piece of the substance or the container it was in.

Cars Can Be Deadly

When William gets in the car, the first thing he does is fasten his seat belt. He's used to it. If I don't fasten mine instantly, he says, "You don't have yours on."

I say, "Okay," and I put it on.

Ruthie Faye, 19 - William, 4; Soraya, 18 months

Cars can be deadly for toddlers. If he's in the car, make sure he's buckled into his car seat. If he weighs 60 pounds or more, or is at least six years old, he can use the regular seat belt. Incidentally, be just as sure that you're buckled in, too. You're his model.

The car seat process is more complicated if you have two children to buckle in. Edie, mother of two-year-old twins, buckles one twin in on the curbside where she can control the other one. She then carefully takes the second one around to the street side to complete the job.

Your toddler moves quickly, but is only now beginning to develop the ability and self-control to stay out of busy streets and to watch for cars as he crosses even a garage driveway. Insist that he hold your hand when you cross a street, go through a parking lot, or across a driveway.

Going in the street — that's a big one. Right away she thinks she can go in the street. One day she ran out, and here comes a car. I screamed at her and spanked her. Since then, she goes up to the curb, she looks, and then she walks away.

I say, "If the ball goes in the street, you come get Mommy," and, "If your friends cross the street, don't follow them. You come to me and I'll help you."

We cross the street together. She's learning. I tell her all the time, "Cars won't see you, Haley," and she'll say, "Okay, Mommy, I'll wait for you."

Bettiann

For a more detailed discussion of making your home safe for your toddler, see *Your Baby's First Year.*

Preventing Serious Illness

Tatiana has had a fever several times, and one time she broke out in hives. I put cortisone on her and left her uncovered for a little while so her fever could drop. The hives went away the next day.

She gets sick quite often, I think because she just started a new day care. She gets sick real easy, so either my mom has to take off or I have to stay home from school to take care of her.

Mihaela, 16 - Tatiana, 18 months

Your child should see your healthcare provider for a checkup about every nine to twelve months during his second and third years. Before you go to the doctor, write down your questions. It's easy to forget them when you're face to face with your super-busy doctor.

You've probably made sure your toddler got his twelve immunizations on schedule during his first year. When he's 18 months old, he needs to go back for "refills."

At 12-15 months she'll need to be immunized against rubella (German measles), mumps, and red measles (MMR). She should also have a skin test for tuberculosis at that time. Your healthcare provider may also recommend she receive the chickenpox (varicella) vaccine sometime during her second year.

Your Baby Needs a Doctor

Celeste and Carrie have gotten real sick this winter. We've been to the doctor like ten times. I don't take them outside, I give them vitamins, but one gets sick, and then the other one.

What do I do when they get sick? I call my grandma. If she can't help, I take them to the doctor and get medicine. When they're sick, they sleep quite a bit, but they both want to be held together. It's real hard.

Noelle-Marie, 19 - Celeste, 21/2; Carrie, 9 months

If you don't have a healthcare provider for your child, call your local health department. They will give you the name of a doctor and/or tell you of a health department clinic where your child can get a health examination.

Should you have any questions regarding your child's health, be sure to check with your healthcare provider. Write down your observations in advance. They may help your doctor make a diagnosis.

Regular check-

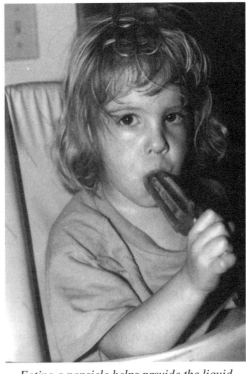

Eating a popsicle helps provide the liquid she needs if she has a fever or is nauseous.

ups are a good time to ask questions about your child's health and about his growth and development. Talk with your healthcare provider about caring for a sick child at home. Ask what to give for a fever. How high should your child's temperature be before you call the doctor? Is there a cough syrup to keep on hand? How about allergy medicines?

Your child's vision and hearing will be checked as part of his well-baby examination. Any other examinations by specialists should be done only if recommended by your healthcare provider.

Diarrhea Is Still Dangerous

When your child was an infant, you knew how dangerous diarrhea could be. You probably called your doctor soon after the diarrhea started because you didn't want your baby to become dehydrated. Diarrhea is still a dangerous condition for your child. Because it causes dehydration, diarrhea can be a very serious problem for toddlers, too.

The two most important things in caring for the child with diarrhea are:

- Give lots of liquids.
- Give little or no fat-containing foods such as French fries or butter.

When Your Child Gets Sick

Haley got strep throat once when I did. She was about 14 months old, and I was trying to take care of her by myself.

My mom and dad were gone on vacation, and I was scared and didn't know what to do. She was feverish, and I kept her in the bathtub for a long time.

Then my aunt came over and said, "You're going to

*the doctor." She took us both in, and he prescribed
antibiotics for both of us. That was a terrible week.*

Bettiann

Doctors often give antibiotics such as penicillin. It is
very important to give *all* of the medicine to your child so
the illness doesn't return in a week or two. Sometimes
moms think they can save some medicine to use the next
time the child is sick. This is not smart.

If not all the germs are killed, those that remain are
likely to become resistant to the antibiotic. Next time your
child has a similar illness, the antibiotic may not work. To
repeat, give your child *all* the medicine prescribed.

Colds are difficult in the preschool years. Attending
school is usually a nice experience for the child but unfor-
tunately, she is likely to get one or two more colds. The
first year the child attends any school, this is likely to
happen. If the parent waits until she's ready for kindergarten, it will probably happen then.

*He had a cough when I took him in for his checkup.
The doctor said to put the vaporizer on at night, and
that seems to help. He's getting better.*

Evangelina, 18 - Ricardo, 31/2; Raul, 27 months

A cold-water vaporizer is a good investment. Using it in
your child's room will help him breathe more easily when
he's congested. Some children have a particularly rough
time with asthma and/or allergies:

*Luke gets sick often, mostly coughs and congestion.
I think it's allergies. The doctor said it may develop
into asthma. They have to give him antibiotics.*

*He got a real high fever once, and I put him in the
bathtub with cool water. He was crying, but my mom
was there to help me.*

Ashley

Having *their* mother's help when their child is sick is very reassuring for many young parents.

Ear Infections Must Be Treated

Abby had an ear infection last week. I could tell because she's usually a real active baby, but she only wanted to sit on my lap.

She was pulling at her ear, and I said, "Abby, does your ear hurt?" She nodded. Of course I took her to the doctor.

Ashley

If your child appears to have an ear infection, *call the doctor.* Untreated ear infections, in addition to being quite painful, can easily cause loss of hearing. A child who can't hear well misses out on a lot, and is likely to have a difficult time when he starts school.

If he can't hear, he will have a hard time learning to talk. He won't hear how words should sound. His language will sound garbled and be hard to understand.

Most ear infections, if caught soon enough, can be treated with no lasting problem.

Ellie had a lot of ear infections that first year. Then we realized she wasn't talking, and our friends' babies were talking a lot. We took her to an ear, nose and throat doctor, and he said, "She can't hear."

We sat in a room where a little monkey rang a bell. Ellie wouldn't even look when he rang the bell.

I felt so bad when I found out she was deaf. We had yelled at her, "Ellie, come here," and she wouldn't respond. Then we'd get mad at her.

They did surgery on her ears, and she's hearing fine now. Two days after the surgery I said, "Ellie," and she looked at me. A couple of days later she was

saying "Mommy" for the first time. She also likes
music now. She couldn't hear it before.

Shalimar, 19 - Ellie, 30 months

For a more detailed discussion on your child's health
care, see *Your Baby's First Year.*

Caring for Toddler's Teeth

Your toddler may have had no trouble cutting his early
teeth. His first and second molars, which come through
during his second year, can be a different matter. He may
be quite miserable and irritable when these molars are
coming through his gums.

Some things you can do to help include giving him
something cold to bite on, using a teething cream, or giving
a pain medication (such as Tylenol) when he's miserable.
He may like to play with ice cubes. Even rubbing his gums
with your finger
may help, if only to
let him know
you're trying to do
something for him.

If he seems to be
in a lot of pain, it
may not be his
teeth. If he keeps
putting his hand up
to the side of his
face, perhaps he has
an earache. Check
with his doctor.

Your toddler
needs his own
toothbrush. You

Be sure to take good care of his baby teeth.   should be brushing his teeth as soon as three or four teeth have erupted. Now he will want to help, but be sure his teeth are brushed thoroughly at least twice a day.

The easiest way to show him how to brush is to stand him in front of you with the back of his head against you. Brace his head against one hand and brush with the other. Show him how to brush the upper teeth down and the lower teeth up, the way they grow. You'll need to supervise his brushing for several years yet.

Those baby teeth have three important uses:

- They help him move from only milk to solid foods he can chew.
- Baby teeth help shape the child's jaw.
- They help him pronounce words correctly.

For these reasons, you need to take your toddler in for a dental checkup by age 3. If there are cavities, it's important to have them filled.

Keeping your child safe and healthy during her toddler years is an important part of your parenting career. It's up to you to create a safe environment for her. It's up to you to care for her when she's ill. It's also up to you to guide her toward eating the good foods and getting the rest she needs for optimal health.

As you already know, parenting provides lots of challenges. Your reward for meeting these challenges is your child's well-being and love.

Both boys and girls need to be protected from abuse.

11

Protecting Your Child From Sexual Abuse

- Teen Parents and Sexual Abuse
- Sexual Abuse Is Devastating
- Protecting Your Child from Abuse
- Heart to Heart Program
- Does Abuse Affect One's Parenting?
- "I Finally Told My Mom"
- Who Do You Tell?
- Getting Professional Help

When I was 3, I was molested, and when I was 10, I was raped by my mother's boyfriend. Sometimes I find myself getting frustrated real easily because I have a lot of flashbacks. On Saturday I had a real bad flashback, and it hurts Dorian's dad to see me go through that.

My boyfriend was the first person I told. Then I finally told my mom. I didn't speak up sooner because I thought my family would turn on me, and they did. They blamed me.

I finally told my mom's boyfriend, when I was 11, "Stop, don't touch me. Get away from me." Other than that, I think he would have continued it for years.

I'm learning to be more honest now. I feel like there's a big weight lifted from my shoulders. So many girls have gone through it, especially those in parenting classes.

Denae, 16 - Dorian, 11 months

Teen Parents and Sexual Abuse

I was sexually abused by my brother. My mother doesn't know. I was only like 3 or 4, and I remember all these things that my brother used to do to me. Now I'm getting on with my life. I don't talk to my brother. People say you're lucky, you have boys, and you don't have to worry about that. But you do.

Kerrianne, 19 - Sergy, 3; Leonardo, 4

Many teen mothers have been sexually abused. In fact, according to research, a majority have faced some degree of abuse as they were growing up. Abuse happens to boys, too, and teen fathers have been abused.

Sexual abuse happened to my husband. My husband never said anything until he was older, and then nobody believed him. It happened when he was 6, and he talked about it when he was 12.

Doug told me he thought I wouldn't like him because of what happened to him. I told him I love him for who he is, not for what somebody did to him.

I don't know how to protect Caelin.

Alaina, 17 - Caelin, 4 months

Victims of sexual abuse are likely to blame themselves. The child feels violated, but s/he may not tell anyone. The abuser usually either tells them, "This is our little secret," or threatens harm to them or their family if they tell.

Sexual Abuse Is Devastating

Kaye was molested by her grandfather when she was very young. Then, when she was 14, her sister-in-law's brother raped her. She commented:

> *It is the most devastating thing. My sister-in-law still doesn't understand, and it was her brother who was the minister who raped me. She still sees it as sex, but it is not sex when I was 14 and he was 28. Just the devastation, the damage it does, they do not understand at all. Even my husband at times doesn't understand. He wants me to be sexual with him. "Why do you have these hang-ups?"*
>
> *It's very hard to understand unless you have been through it. I look at it as murder. Sexual abuse takes some things you can never get back. It takes so much away from you, and piece by piece you have to try to get it back if you can.*
>
> Kaye, 25 - Wade, 11; Dirk, 8; Tanya, 5

Protecting Your Children from Abuse

> *When I give Karena a bath, I say, "These are your private parts, and you don't let anybody touch them. If somebody does, please tell Mommy. You won't get in trouble, and Mommy needs to know."*
>
> *You need to let the child know she can come to her mother for anything. She can tell mother if something bad happens.*
>
> *If kids have secure feelings basically, that's a big protection.*
>
> Yoko, 25 - Sheila, 9; Matthew, 6; Karena, 2

Whether or not you've been abused, you want to do all you can to protect your child, whether a girl or a boy. One in four females and about one in seven males in the United

States will be sexually abused or raped before age 20. The majority of those committing the abuse are known to their victims.

Some women sexually abuse children, but most of the time the abusers are males. He could be a stranger, but he's more likely to be someone the child knows. He may be a friend of the family, an uncle, cousin, stepfather, mom's boyfriend, or even the biological father.

We often tell children, "Don't talk to strangers." But this doesn't take care of the problem since the abuser may have a close relationship with the child.

Some children are taught that adults are always right. They are to respect adults and obey them. Yet no one, adult or child, is always right. And there are adults who are not worthy of a child's respect. Your child needs to know s/he has the right to say "No" to another person, whatever their age.

When you're discussing good touch and bad touch with your children, use concrete examples. Petting your kitty is a good touch. If the cat scratches you, that's a bad touch. If someone you like very much gives you a hug, that's a good touch. However, if you get a funny feeling about that hug, maybe it's a bad touch. Or if your uncle gives you a hug, and that feels good, but he does something else that feels different, is that a good touch or a bad touch?

Children can understand the difference between good touch and bad touch. You might add that sometimes a doctor may need to examine them, but in that case, you should be there with them. A good doctor welcomes a parent being there during a child's physical examination.

An important point you make with your children is that they can talk to you about anything. They should never feel embarrassed or ashamed when they talk to you.

Teach them the correct names for body parts. If they

don't think they should say the words penis and vagina, how can they tell you somebody asked them to touch it?

No one should force affection on a child. Your child has a right to say "No," even when grandpa wants to kiss her or tickle her. Grandpa may be hurt, but you can help him understand that today Jessica doesn't feel like being hugged or tickled. Jessica needs to know, no matter how little she is, that she doesn't hug or kiss anyone unless she wants to.

Heart to Heart Program

A couple of years after her first son was born, Kaye participated in the Heart to Heart Program. This program, developed by the Ounce of Prevention Fund based in Chicago, teaches teen parents how they can protect themselves and their children from sexual abuse. Kaye explained:

> *Heart to Heart helped me learn how to protect my children. It made me deal with my own sexual abuse. I was walking around with blinders on just like my mom. I learned so much from that program, and I brought it home to the kids.*
>
> *My son was 2 when I went through Heart to Heart. I think the key thing is to talk about abuse. It's not a taboo thing, something you talk about only in secret. We talk openly and freely.*
>
> *The same way you say, "Don't touch that stove, it's hot," you say, "Don't let anybody touch your private areas." They need to know that somebody they love can hurt them.*
>
> *When I was growing up, it was like it would be somebody jumping out of an alley, but that wasn't the way it was. It could be your father, your grandfather, your uncles. Children need the information to protect*

themselves in that family setting instead of always
hearing about people off the street.

Even at this age, I think they understand between
good touches and bad touches. They are affectionate
with others in the family.

My daughter is good at speaking up. Somebody will
come up to her and say, "Give me a hug, give me a
kiss," and she will say "No," and that's all right. You
have to respect children's wishes.

A lot of times sexual abuse happens because the
child needs attention. That's not what they want, but
it's like the child who is abused physically. He will
still love that person anyway because it's some kind of
attention.

I'm still very very concerned about my grandfather.
Other kids are over there, but my kids aren't at all.
And that hurts because I would like my kids to have a
relationship with my grandmother.

Kaye

Does Abuse Affect One's Parenting?

Kaye talked about the lingering effects of her abuse. Her
sons are now 11 and 8, and her daughter is 5. In spite of her
efforts to go on with her life, she says the abuse has made
a difference.

First, she explained that her first pregnancy, when she
was 13, was very much because of the abuse. She had not
been allowed to make decisions about her own sexuality.
She was not a real partner in what was happening. So one
day she made a choice, and had sex with the boy across the
street. She conceived, and, in spite of her family's horror at
the pregnancy, for her it was a positive thing:

From the very beginning I accepted my pregnancy.
I needed that baby, and the pregnancy stopped the

*abuse for awhile. Pretty much it kept me safe. I had
begun to feel very worthless, very abnormal, low self-
esteem. I felt very misused. Having that baby made me
feel loved again. It made me feel like I had a purpose
in life. So I welcomed the pregnancy.*

Kaye also talked about the negative effects her abuse has
had on her parenting.

*At times I feel like I'm not as physical with my kids.
With my boys, I hug and I kiss them, but sometimes I
push them away because I don't want any sexual
overtones there. I have more freedom with my daughter. When my boys want to sit on my lap, I can't deal
with it. Even at times, bathing them when they were
little, I was real uncomfortable. I think that's the
negative.*

*Sometimes I can push them away when I feel like
it's too much. But they need the affection just as much
as my daughter does. I put a space between us, and I
wish that wasn't there.*

To parent a child well, a parent needs to feel secure and
have high self-esteem. In studies of victims of sexual
abuse, the victims score low on self-worth. They have a
higher rate of depression, and of drug and alcohol abuse.

If the parent can't feel good about her/himself, it will be
difficult to raise a child with good self-esteem. You can't
give someone something you don't have.

"I Finally Told My Mom"

*You need to talk about it. First you need to be
honest with yourself. Recognize that it did happen.
You have to be real with yourself. I was going off the
handle. For sanity's sake, you have to tell somebody.*

Denae

If this has happened to you, are you talking to someone about your experiences? Too often, sexual abuse is suffered in silence. It's considered a taboo subject, yet the abuser, if not reported, will most likely continue by abusing someone else. Victims wonder if their stories would be believed. Or they don't want to disrupt family relationships.

> *I finally told my mom about my grandfather be-*
> *cause I couldn't stand it happening any more.*
> *My mother took this very hard. She almost had a*
> *nervous breakdown. This made her deal with her own*
> *abuse. My grandfather had sexually abused her when*
> *she was a child, too. She had a lot of guilt that if she*
> *had exposed him way back then, he wouldn't have had*
> *the opportunity to get to me.*
>
> Kaye

Dealing with a daughter's (or son's) sexual abuse is, of course, difficult for a mother. She may blame herself, as Kaye's mother did, because she had not shared the nightmare of her own sexual abuse. In other families, the mother may have known about the abuse, or at least the victim thinks she did. Then why didn't Mom protect her? Denae continues to wonder:

> *I have a lot of hard feelings toward my mom. Until*
> *recently she was visiting her boyfriend in jail, yet he*
> *confessed to all of this (abuse). I started going to ther-*
> *apy once he turned himself in. I can't afford to freak*
> *out because it would be Dorian who would suffer.*
>
> Denae

Who Do You Tell?

If you've been abused and you haven't gotten help, haven't talked to anyone about it, you'd probably be wise to talk to someone. If you can't talk to your mother, start with a friend, an aunt, perhaps a counselor at school. Find somebody you can trust.

You need to find someone who really understands the dynamics of abuse, and that *the abuse was not your fault.* Kaye discovered sometimes the conversation would turn around to "What did you do?" She said:

> *If someone puts the blame on you, know absolutely it's not your fault. After my grandfather was arrested, the police officer told me that even if a prostitute stands out in the street naked, nobody has the right to touch her unless she permits it. That helped me a lot.*
>
> Kaye

Getting Professional Help

Because an abused person generally has so many questions and doubts, s/he may need to find professional help. It's important to find a counselor who understands the dynamics of sexual abuse, how it can affect other aspects of your life, especially your parenting.

If you don't know who to call in your area, call the Sexual Assault Crisis Agency for Victims hotline, 562/597-2002. Someone there should be able to refer you to a counselor and/or suggest where to go for help in your area. Also, in many states, according to Jan Stanton, former director of Heart to Heart, the YWCA and the YMCA provide help for sexual abuse victims.

If none of these sources help, call the Ounce of Prevention's Heart to Heart Program in Chicago, 312/922-3863, and ask where to go in your area for the help you need.

Whether you're trying to recover from the abuse you've endured, or you're determined to protect your child from abuse — or both — you have an important task. *More power to you!*

A satisfying partnership takes lots of love, respect, and caring.

12

The Partnership Challenge

I'm still young, I want to have friends, and I'd like to go out. It's frustrating for Nathan, too, because rarely do we go out by ourselves.

Things change. I used to say, "Oh, I'm so in love." I still love him, but . . . I'm stressed sometimes so much that it's, "Oh, what do you want?"

Before I got pregnant, I thought everything would be so easy — the baby is so cute, and we're a little family, but it's not quite that way.

We're trying to keep our relationship going, but I feel so far away from him. He works

*4 a.m.-1 p.m., then sleeps until 8 or 9. Then he gets
up, but I'm tired and I go to bed. But we both realize
Dakota needs two parents.*

Zandra, 16 - Dakota, 11 months

*Usually we stay home with Dakota. We get out
once in awhile, not often. That hurts our relationship
because Zandra likes to go out.*

*Sometimes it seems like we're drifting apart. We
don't see each other much. About the only time I see
Zandra is when I pick her up at school.*

Nathan, 20 - Dakota, 11 months

Parenting Alone

Many teenage mothers are rearing their toddlers alone.
The baby's father may have vanished when he learned the
young woman was pregnant. Or they may have stayed
together throughout pregnancy, perhaps longer, then ended
their relationship.

If you're parenting alone, you're probably working very
hard and, if you're like many other single parents, you'd
rather be sharing your parenting responsibilities.

If you're with your baby's other parent, however, or with
a different partner, you probably face some problems in
parenting together. Good relationships take time, effort, and
energy in addition to love just as good parenting takes time,
effort, and energy in addition to lots of love.

It's hard to parent alone, but it's also difficult to fit in
enough time and effort for both your partner and your
child. Making good decisions concerning partners is perhaps one of the hardest issues faced by teenage parents.
There is likely to be even more heartbreak in a failed
relationship when there is a child involved.

Teenage parents of toddlers tend to be involved in a
variety of relationships. Only one in five teenage mothers is

married when her child is born. By the time the child is three, a high percentage of these marriages have ended. By this time, many teenage parents are with a different partner.

Will You Love Again?

I'm very cautious with the guys I go out with. If he doesn't like Chandler, even if he's the nicest guy in the world, it's good-bye.

Gretchen, 17 - Chandler, 13 months

Sometimes a single teenage mother may wonder if she will ever have a love relationship again. If a man knows she has a child, will he want to be with her? Or will she be left alone to parent her child? If he does see her, will their new relationship upset her child? Elysha is typical of many teen mothers who say this isn't a problem for them:

My having a child doesn't bother anyone. I had thought a lot of young men would think, "Well, you have a child so I won't bother." But a lot of the guys I know are attached to Antoine.

"Can Antoine come with us?" they ask. Sometimes we include him.

The only time I date are the weekends. I work eight hours a day, then pick up my child at school. We do what we have to do at home, we go to bed, and then we start the day again.

Elysha, 21 - Antoine, 4

Sometimes it's hard for a toddler to understand why mom leaves her to go out with her boyfriend:

When a boyfriend comes to pick me up, Susie decides she wants to go. She puts her clothes on and follows me out to the car. We try to explain, "Mommy is going out, and you have to stay home."

*My mom usually picks Susie up and brings her in
the house. She cries until she realizes Mom will come
home later. Then she goes to bed.*

Cathi, 18 - Susie, 34 months

If Cathi talked with Susie ahead of time about her plans
for the evening, Susie might be more accepting. Perhaps
Cathi could do something special with Susie before she
goes out. If Cathi's date means she won't be able to read
Susie a bedtime story, perhaps they could have a reading
session earlier in the day.

Is Marriage a Solution?

*I think Jenae has brought us more together, my
partner and I. Now that we have her, it's like, "Okay,
if we're going to spend time together, and since we
don't leave her, we need to have more time for me and
you to talk." I think that's important. There's a lot of
trust and a lot of communication. I think that's why
we've been together for a long time, four years.*

*I want to wait until I'm 18 to get married. Mar-
riage is not a thing to play around with. It's important, something you live with for the rest of your life.*

Clancy Jane, 17 - Jenae, 23 months

Some parenting couples stay together, but choose not to
marry during pregnancy, or perhaps not for months or even
years after their baby is born. Many of these young couples
live together. At first, they are likely to be with his parents
or hers because they can't afford a place of their own. By
the time their child is a toddler, they may have their own
apartment.

However, Rosemarie's parents insisted she and Dick
marry immediately after they learned the young couple was
pregnant. Rosemarie and Dick lived with Rosemarie's

parents for a year. Their relationship didn't go well, and they were delighted when they were finally able to get an apartment by themselves.

Like many other teenage couples, Rosemarie and Dick thought moving out on their own would solve their problems. This didn't happen:

> *Moving out didn't solve our problems. We were fighting more and more.*
>
> *Then one day Dick hit me, and that did it. My father used to knock us around when I was little. I vowed that when I grew up, nobody was going to hit me. I had warned Dick I'd leave if he ever hit me. So I did.*
>
> Rosemarie, 19 - Helen, 3

Sadly, violence is a part of many teenage (and older) relationships. It takes a great deal of courage for a woman to walk out of such a relationship, especially if she has no money and no place to go. Rosemarie at least had a high school education and some job skills. She continued her story:

> *To be perfectly honest, right after my divorce, I didn't know how we would survive. But I didn't have a choice. I couldn't live with him. Now I'm trying to put my life back together, and I'm adjusting pretty well.*
>
> *Helen and I are living with my sister and her husband and their baby. We can't afford a decent apartment by ourselves, so I split living expenses with them. I couldn't handle living with my parents now because they would try to take over. Being with my sister is a little different because we're peers.*
>
> Rosemarie

If you're in an abusive relationship, do everything you can to get out of it. *You don't deserve to be hit!* Check the phone book or ask your school counselor or your social worker for information about women's shelters in your area, shelters which take women and children.

You might find reading *Breaking Free from Partner Abuse* by Mary Marecek helpful. (See Appendix.) Included are vignettes of women in abusive relationships together with suggestions for escaping such a relationship. Also see *Baby Help* by Marilyn Reynolds, a novel about Melissa, a teen mom living with her abusive boyfriend.

Divorce Is Difficult

For some married couples, divorce may be the best solution to a lot of unhappiness. But divorce is seldom easy.

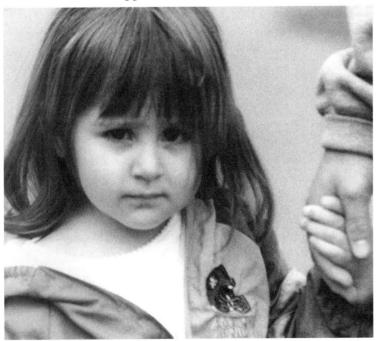

It's important to her that Mom and Dad have a good relationship.

Sometimes marriage counseling *before* divorce can help a couple work through their problems. Divorce is seldom easy for either partner, and it's almost always hard on the children involved. Divorce doesn't solve problems. It's the people involved who must solve those problems. For some, divorce may be a necessary step, but it won't be easy.

Making the Marriage Decision

Whether you've never been married, or you're divorced, you may be considering marriage now. If you are, you and your partner may want to discuss such things as:

- Do you both want to spend the rest of your life together?

- Is one of you working and earning enough to support your family? If only one is working, is s/he willing to support the other one and your child?

- Do you have a place to live? For most couples, it's harder to develop a good relationship while you're living with other people.

- Do your answers agree on such important questions as:

  - When will you have your next child?

  - Will either or both of you continue going to school?

  - Who is expected to have a job? Husband? Wife? Both?

  - Who will take primary responsibility for the care of your child?

You can think of a lot of other things you need to discuss thoroughly before you decide to spend the rest of your lives together.

Trust is an important factor in a good relationship. Many young people, not yet quite sure of their own worth, have problems with jealousy. If he's out without her, he must have a girlfriend. If she's out with her girlfriends, he's sure she's getting in trouble. Domingo talked about this issue:

I feel trust is the #1 thing you need in a relationship. If you feel you can't trust your significant other, you should just get out of the relationship.

I feel I can talk to Lupe. Some of my friends ask me why I "let" her go hang out with her friends. And she trusts me. My friends also say, "Oh, I don't ask her (if I can go out) because she would never let me. I just go out." We have time away from each other, and we don't have to ask why or what.

It's really a negative effect on the relationship if a guy can't trust his girl or a girl can't trust her man. You can't share your money with someone unless you trust each other. It has to work both ways.

You trust this person to help raise your kid. You trust this person to help feed you. You always have to be able to count on this person.

Some people say they trust their girl, but when she takes off for the mall, he asks her, "Who did you see? What did you do?" That sours the whole thing.

If you trust somebody, you shouldn't have no jealousy. You develop that trust. You want to trust your kid to behave right, and you want to have that trust in your child's mother. It's a sad issue not to trust somebody.

Domingo, 22 - Lorenzo, 4

The two of you might like to read *Teenage Couples: Caring, Commitment and Change* and *Teenage Couples: Coping with Reality* (Lindsay) together. You'll find a lot of suggestions for making a partnership work, whether you're married or simply living with your partner.

At the back of *Caring, Commitment and Change* is a "Score Card" for teenage marriage decisions. You and your partner might each like to take this "test," then compare your answers. It might help you see more clearly the areas in which you agree and those in which you disagree.

A fairly long questionnaire concerning attitudes toward marriage and living together is in *Coping with Reality*. Completing the questionnaire together is also an excellent way to help you start talking about some important issues. Too often, partners don't communicate well about money, children, families, home preferences, career goals, and other vitally important topics.

Making a Good Partnership Better

It was hard because he went to work, and we both went to school, but on the weekends we would talk. If something bothers us, we talk about it and go from there.

Me and my parents didn't have much communication, and neither did his parents before they got divorced. We decided talking about things was better than arguing about it and just getting mad.

Alaina, 17 - Caelin, 4 months

The relationship with your partner may be more complicated because you're a parent. If it's a poor relationship, you may, because of your child, not feel free to leave. If your partner is not your child's father, you may worry about the effect this situation will have on your toddler.

If you're with a partner, you probably would like your relationship to be as good as possible. One thing to remember is that it's important that neither partner feel put down or badly treated by the other.

Sometimes people talk about a good relationship being a

50-50 situation — each partner has equal rights and responsibilities. A better percentage is probably 60-60 — each
partner goes *more* than half way to please the other. At the
same time, each partner needs to realize how important s/he
is, and be willing to guard his/her own self-esteem while
doing more than his/her share in maintaining a loving and
caring relationship with the partner.

> *No matter how bad things get or how hard, we
> have to do our best to keep our family together. We
> have to think about Buchanan. We want to raise him
> the right way with a mother and a father, so we have
> committed that we are going to be together.*
>
> *When we get in fights . . . like before when we'd
> fight, one of us would say, "Well, I'm going to leave
> you." But we made an agreement that when we get
> angry with each other, we aren't going to say that.*
>
> *We agree that if one of us is angry, we'll show love.
> We'll say, "Come here, baby, let me hug you."*
>
> Camelia, 16 - Buchanan, 6 months

Maintaining a good relationship is not easy. It takes a lot
of nurturing, but, for many, it is worth the effort. Living
within a good partnership can make parenting even more
satisfying.

Winning Over the Other Parents

When you and your partner have a child together, getting
along with the other grandparents is usually important, both
for your child and for your peace of mind. Whether or not
you live with your partner's parents, you probably want
your child to be able to enjoy his grandparents. Sometimes
those grandparents need to be won over:

> *When she learned I was pregnant, Stan's mother
> told him not to see me again, to give the baby up and*

go into the Marines as he had planned. "Don't let her interfere," she told him.

The first time I saw Stan's mom was at the hospital because she didn't want her neighbors to know I was pregnant. She didn't want her family to know, and she didn't want her church to know. She wanted me to stay out of sight.

Stan and I decided to get married a couple of months after Ryan was born. His mother tried to plan our wedding. I think the closest we ever came to splitting was when I put my foot down and said, "If you want to plan this wedding with your mother, then marry your mother. If you want to marry me, we'll plan it together."

Kristin, 23 - Ryan, 8; Tiana, 4

Kristin, however, decided she wouldn't accept a poor relationship with her husband's parents. They needed to get along for Ryan's sake, so she took the lead in improving family relationships:

Things started changing after I began taking Ryan over there. I got along good with Stan's brothers and sisters, so I'd pick a time when they'd be home. I would act like it was a normal visit to grandma and grandpa.

Then Stan started going along with me.

I didn't want to explain to Ryan why grandma didn't come to visit. I didn't want him to think grandma didn't come over because she didn't love him. I didn't want him to think grandma didn't like me because I got pregnant with him. So I acted normal, and in the long run, it worked. She respects me.

Nobody wins if you stay away. I don't know how I knew that would be best, but I knew it would be wrong

to drive a bigger wedge, and I didn't want to come
between Stan and his mom.

Kristin

Encouraging positive contact between your child and
both sets of grandparents usually is best for the child and
for the grandparents. Kristin won over her husband's
parents because she was willing to make an effort. At the
time, it would have been easier to say, "They don't like me
and I don't like them. That's all there is to it." Instead, she
was determined that Ryan would win. In the process,
everyone in this family became winners.

Whether you're still living with your parents or you're in
your own home, fostering a good relationship between your
child and his grandparents is important.

Planning Your Family

Right now that's not even in my mind, having
another kid. I think I'm barely learning with this one,
and for me to teach another one, not right now.
Maybe in five years, maybe when I have a job.

Clancy Jane

A lot of teenagers who have one child have another
within one or two years. Often this second pregnancy is not
planned. It may, in fact, create a real hardship for the young
mother:

I didn't want Kerry — it was a total accident. I was
on the pill, but I ran out and was going to wait until
after my period. This pregnancy upset me terribly.
Amy was the only one I wanted. I don't like having
two kids. I thought about abortion, but I knew deep
down I wouldn't do it.

Her father's mom said, "But that's my first grand-

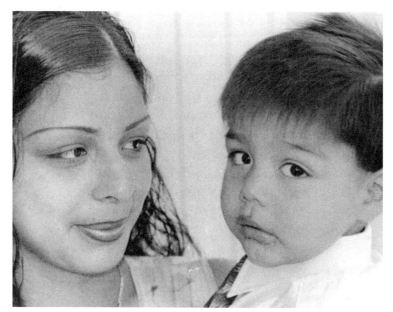

*Both you and your child are more likely to have the life you want
if you don't have your second child too quickly.*

*child," and my mom said, "You won't be welcome in
the family if you do that." That's my whole family.*

Leslie, 20 - Amy, 27 months; Kerry, 4 months

What Are Your Options?

*Once you're pregnant, it's up to you if you have an
abortion or keep it. I don't put anybody down for an
abortion, because if you know you won't be happy
with that child, it's even more tragic to try to raise it.*

*After she has her baby, every girl should find a
birth control method. I think if I get pregnant again, it
will be because I want to. If you're in a relationship
with one person, both of you should take the
responsibility.*

*With one child, I can go ahead and do what I want.
With two or three children and no husband, I'd be*

really limited. I don't want another child until
I'm married.

Shirley, 20 - Virginia, 4

If you aren't pregnant now, you have three options as far as pregnancy is concerned. One is obvious. If you don't have sex, you won't get pregnant. The majority of high school students still choose this method. If you see statistics stating that 25 percent of all 15-year-old girls have had sexual intercourse, that means that 75 percent have not.

Your second option is to use birth control if you're having sexual intercourse. If you don't want another baby, this is essential.

I have a girlfriend who doesn't use birth control
because she says she can't talk about it with her
boyfriend. I tell her if she's too embarrassed to talk to
him, don't have sex with him. The whole idea is
just silly.

Melinda, 15 - Robin, 9 months

Lots of teenagers think, "It won't happen to me. I won't get pregnant." But one couple in 25 will become pregnant at the time of first intercourse. Of the couples having intercourse twelve times without using contraception, *one-half* will become pregnant.

Would you ride in a car if you knew that one-half of those who take twelve rides will have a serious accident? If you aren't ready to have a baby, or if you already have one and aren't ready for another, an unplanned pregnancy is certainly a "serious accident."

If you want to be an independent person, you can't
depend on the man to use birth control. Independence
is important to me — it always has been. If you use
birth control yourself, you know for sure.

Darla, 17 - Janis, 2

You'll find a description of the various methods of birth control in *Your Pregnancy and Newborn Journey.*

Your third option is to get pregnant. If you're having sex and you don't use birth control, this is the option you apparently have chosen.

If you're pregnant now, you still have two options other than raising the child yourself. You can get an abortion, or you can release your child for adoption.

Releasing her child for adoption used to be the accepted "solution" for a pregnant teenager who was not married. Today, however, less than four percent of unmarried pregnant adolescents choose adoption for their child. Yet this could be the most loving, caring decision a birthmother could make. For more information on adoption, and for personal accounts of young mothers who chose this option, see Lindsay's *Pregnant? Adoption is an Option.*

Enough Time for First Child

Many young mothers and fathers want to have enough time between their babies to give each child the love and attention he needs. They also realize the expense of having one child, and prefer to wait at least two or three years before having another baby.

There are many reasons to delay your second baby, practical reasons like how will you afford another child? One of the most caring reasons is that you want to have enough time and energy to give your first child the attention he needs. Many young parents feel a toddler is better off being an only child for at least two or three years.

Parenting a child or several children is a wonderful experience. It will be more wonderful if you have the resources — time, money, relationship — that you need to parent well. *Your child and your future children will thank you.*

"I don't want to put my son's life in jeopardy."

13

Gang Involvement Versus Parenting

I've had guns pulled on me, and that wasn't much fun, One time me and Lupe and my son were crossing the street, just walking home from the local park. A car cut us off as we were walking, and I was so upset I flipped the driver off. He decided to come back, himself and two women. He ended up pulling a gun on me. Lupe was pushing my son's stroller, and he was no older than 6 months.

Lupe broke into tears, crying, "Don't shoot him," and I had nothing to say, it was such a shock. The girls in the car kept telling him to get back in the car, and he finally left.

*I thought I'd keep my temper from here on. Some-
one else might react even more. I put my son's life in
jeopardy.*

*Before, when I was in a gang, I could take off
running and not worry about leaving anybody behind.
In this instance, I couldn't just leave.*

Domingo, 22 - Lorenzo, 4

*Where I used to live there are more gangs than
anything else. There's nothing to do over there for
younger people so gangs are especially important. If
you had money, you could hang around with the
football players and stuff, but if you didn't have
money, the gangs were there. I also had a bad
childhood, and I was angry a lot.*

*Getting out — it was like little by little. Someone
real close to me died, and I was there and I saw it. It
woke me up in a lot of ways because I had thought it
was all fun and games. I just didn't think beyond what
I was doing. It was like a reality check.*

*Some people don't get out of the gang because
they're too scared. I knew it wouldn't be easy. I was
afraid, but I'd confront people before they confronted
me. My boyfriend didn't know me when I was
like that.*

*Moving away gave me a chance to get my head
straight. I knew girls who have their babies. They're
still over there gang-banging and beating up people
for what they wear, but they're not real mothers.*

*I'm glad I got out of that gang stuff before Dakota
was born. I had one friend over there, a guy, and he
had a little girl. He was in the wrong place at the
wrong time, and they shot her, killed his little girl,
by mistake.*

Zandra, 16 - Dakota, 11 months

Pregnancy May Be a Way Out

*A lot of my girlfriends, when they got pregnant,
said, "This isn't for me." I think some of my friends
got pregnant because they wanted out of the gang.
Most of their boyfriends are still in the gang, and they
aren't helping the girls support the kid.*

*I tell my little sister, if you get in a gang, we're
packing ourselves up and moving. Because when you
need something, they aren't going to be there for you.
When you need someone to talk to, they're just going
to laugh at you and walk away.*

Bridget, 18 - Barnaby, 6 months

Thousands of young people across the country belong to
gangs. They may join, be jumped in, before they reach their
teens. They join a gang because they want to belong to
something. They want to be part of a group. The support
members give each other can be positive. They may feel
protected from other gangs.

Gang membership also may mean involvement with
alcohol, drugs, stealing, involuntary sex, and violence.
Gang violence is often reported in the newspapers, and
gang members speak of seeing friends killed. Many schools
are not safe for students because of gang activity.

Kelsey considered the gang her family. When her mother
died, her homeboys and homegirls all went to her mom's
funeral. "They kind of supported me," she explained. She
moved in with her stepfather, who was gone on the weekends. The house became the hangout for the gang. After
Kamie was born, however, Kelsey realized something had
to change:

*After I had my daughter, I started calming down,
and my lifestyle changed. I'm tired of people saying,
"The gang is my family. They're there for me when*

*my other family isn't." That's not even true. They're
there if you have a place to party, or if you can get
drugs. We had the house, we had the drugs, we had
the girls. They could come Friday night and Saturday
night and leave Sunday.*

*They were my friends, but where were they when
we got kicked out of the house, where were they when
I needed my mom? When I needed money? The guys,
the partying, all that looks good, but after a while,
you start looking, and you say, "What are they really
doing for you?"*

Kelsey, 19 - Kamie, 21 months

Lucas and Kelsey are living together now, and Lucas
works full-time. He, too, used to be in a gang:

*Before, I would blow off and go down the street
and look for somebody to beat up. That was me, and I
didn't care. But now I have my daughter, and I have
to set an example for her.*

*I started in 7th and 8th grades, and when I got to my
freshman year, I didn't care. I was all into it. But I
still got good grades. I'd always do my homework,
because I still had dreams.*

*I didn't want to be at the same place doing the
same things every day. I didn't want to be in jail, I
didn't want to be strung out on drugs, on the corner
asking for money.*

*Maybe it was seeing what my mom had to go
through. We always were so poor. People would ask
me what we had for dinner, and I didn't want to say
beans and rice. And then my brother, I always saw
him incarcerated, in and out. I decided this had to
stop now in our family.*

Lucas, 21 - Kamie, 21 months

Does Gang Involvement Affect Parenting?

If a gang member becomes pregnant, or is the father of a child, will involvement in the gang have any effect on their child? Is it possible to be a good parent while one is actively involved with a gang? Riley doesn't think so:

> *I have been to meetings with gang members, and they'd bring their kids. They'd be running around listening to what we said. We have all our guns, walking around, drinking, playing with the other kids, smoking weed, and the homeboys, the fathers, don't care. But at the time you don't really think about it because it's not your kids.*
>
> *If I pounded somebody's face in, or I hit him with something, or he's in the hospital, or I left him there to die, just because he's from a different neighborhood, I looked and thought, this is somebody's baby even if he is my age.*
>
> *I looked at my son and thought, will he be like me?*

"Now I can't just think of myself, I have my son to think of."

*I thought, I might lose my son because of gang vio-
lence. My whole family is involved in the gang, my
mother, my father, my uncles. I thought to myself,
things have to change. Dorian is the next generation.
He's the one who's going to school to learn, not be on
the outside doing something wrong.*

*Now I can't just think of myself, I have my son to
think of. I have a beautiful baby, and he needs a lot of
love. When I don't have a job, I feel so bad. I come
close to thinking of going out there and robbing,
selling drugs, but things always come through. I like
my new lifestyle now. I go to work, and I bring a
pretty good sized paycheck home. Everything is going
well right now, and we're getting married next year.*
                                          Riley, 18 - Dorian, 11 months

Sometimes within the gang, a toddler is treated like a pet
or a toy. Gang members may give little thought to his needs
or even his safety. The love and nurturing the child needs
may be hard to get.

Gangs vary a great deal, so it's hard to generalize. Many
young people, however, decide parenthood is a reason to
leave. Sheleen explained why she's no longer with
her gang:

*I realized I wasn't getting anywhere, doing things
like that. It wasn't helping me in any way, just being
with my friends. I walked away from all those people.
I told them I have to take care of my son.*

*My baby's father was in the gang, and he's in jail
now. I don't want anything to do with him.*

*I wouldn't want Brandt to join a gang when he's
older. There's a lot of bad things that can happen to
him, doing stuff like that. He could get killed.*
                                          Sheleen, 15 - Brandt, 1

Some people walk away from their gang without big problems. Others face being jumped out. Theo explained her situation:

> *When I realized I was pregnant, I stopped doing crazy things. I stopped stealing and doing setups because I was pregnant. When Nicklaus was four months old, I called my homeboys, and I said, "I want out."*
>
> *We were at Mousey's house, and they jumped me out. They took me in the other room and got my face bad. My baby didn't hear me crying or yelling, but it was like he was scared. They brought him out five minutes after. When they brought him out, he didn't say anything, it was like he sensed that I was sad. It was like a "Are you OK?" kind of look.*
>
> *I don't want my son to be like that at all. I don't even want him to wear baggy jeans or ever shave his head, or have anything to do with violence.*
>
> Theo, 19 - Nicklaus, 9 months

Theo realizes now that, if this was something she had to do, it would have been far better to leave Nicklaus with her mother or a friend during this time. Babies and gangs don't mix well. In fact, even a very young baby is affected deeply by the violence around him.

> *It's not a good thing for people to hurt other people when they're around their babies. People should realize that their babies are going to remember it for the rest of their lives.*
>
> Francella, 19 - 7 months pregnant

When a gang member decides to leave, it's probably wise to assure members s/he is not rejecting them. S/he just can't handle the action or take the risks anymore. It's usually not necessary to reject them as people, as relatives, or even as friends.

Why Join a Gang?

You get involved in the gangs for the affection, for the love, you get involved for the power, you get involved because of the territory. You realize you have a lot of back-up when you open your mouth. You take a chance, and it doesn't matter until that chance gets caught up with you.

Lonnie, 16 - 8 months pregnant

Several young people explained their reasons for joining a gang. Generally, they felt their own family wasn't there for them.

Dad may have been gone for as long as they can remember. Mom may have been too busy trying to keep the family together, and didn't have time or energy left for them.

Why do kids join gangs? Maybe they aren't getting enough attention from their families, and they want to be with their friends. Maybe they have no one to talk to, no one that's like them and wants to do the things they want to do.

Why did I join? I thought it was fun, going out with my friends. I don't know, it was just the thing to do. I think if I had not been pregnant, I would still be in it.

I think parents of a child should not be in a gang. If you're in a gang, you can have a lot of enemies, and people don't really care if you're with your baby. They may want to start something. If girls don't like my friend (who's in a gang), they really don't care if she has her baby with her.

Sheleen

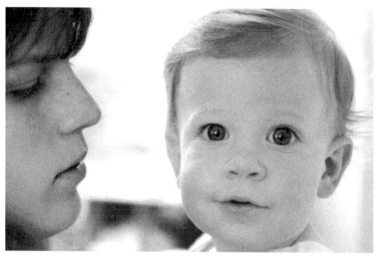

*If he gets plenty of attention from his parents,
he's less likely to choose the gang life.*

The poverty may be overwhelming. In some areas, few activities are available for young people, and the gang appears to fill that need.

> *When you're in an area that doesn't have money, and people are mad and frustrated, it's more likely to happen.*
>
> *I feel like I only joined the gang for attention. My mom was always working, and she's not the kind of person who shows her feelings. She was just there. I think if I would have gotten the attention I needed, I wouldn't have looked somewhere else. The gang was like a second family.*
>
> *A lot of kids feel this way, that nobody else is there for them. I think people who get out of it kind of just grew up. It's not a way of life. It's a sad way of life.*
>
> *That's why I'm going to get an education. I'm not going to depend on someone else to support me.*
>
> Zandra

Riley is quoted earlier in this chapter. He says, *"I thought to myself things have to change. My son is the next generation."* His partner explained why she thinks Riley had joined a gang:

> *Riley grew up without a father. His dad used to beat on his mom. His dad has been in and out of prison. His stepdad is off and on with drugs, so Riley has never had a strong male role model. He felt dumb because kids would make fun of him. He wanted friends real bad, so he got jumped into a gang.*
>
> *He never got out of the gang. He just stopped hanging around. You don't owe them an explanation. You just move on with your life.*
>
> *We both want what's best for Dorian. We want him to have what we didn't have, a good home, with a stable relationship.*
>
> Denae, 16 - Dorian, 11 months

Gang Clothes on Babies?

> *I don't agree with gang clothes on babies. I don't agree with shaved heads on babies. If you want to cut their hair, do that cute little bowl haircut. When they bald their heads, it doesn't look proper, it's not cute. They're babies.*
>
> Samantha, 16 - Kaylie, 20 months

Babies and toddlers tend to be charming little people who generally look good, no matter what they're wearing. Most parents, however, enjoy dressing their children as attractively as possible. Many parents like their children to dress somewhat as they do. A toddler on a farm, for example, might wear overalls or jeans most of the time. A child living on the beach may wear a swimsuit the same color as her mother's. Another toddler's shirt may match his dad's.

He doesn't need to wear gang clothes.

Small children love to mimic their parents, and they usually think it's great if they're wearing clothes similar to mom's or dad's.

Does this extend to gang attire? The young parents we interviewed don't think so.

> *I believe the way you dress is the way you carry yourself. People who dress their kids in gang clothes, it's not right. It's true, you get stereotyped whether it's right or not. And I don't want somebody to come by and shoot them because of what they wear. There are sick people out there. A guy in my block got shot because he was wearing a red hat.*
>
> Kerrianne, 19 - Sergy, 3; Leonardo, 4

Sergy and Leonardo's father continued the discussion:

> *I try not to dress my kids like gang people. I don't want them to be judged because of the way they're dressed. The way you dress kids is an indication of*

how you want them to grow up.

*In our society, clothes make a difference. I have
noticed a lot of people, just because they're dressed in
baggy clothes, they're thought of as gang members.*

*As you get older, common sense will tell you the
gang is not getting you anywhere. Those kids are not
going to put food on your table or a roof over
your head.*

Glen, 25 - Sergy, 3; Leonardo, 4

Will Your Child Join a Gang?

*When I first got pregnant, it was like, yes, I'm
pregnant, no big deal. But when I got my sonogram,
and I saw this person, then I started thinking. Do I
want people saying, "Your son is in a gang" or "Your
son shot my son"? I thought, I still have a chance.*

Vivienne, 19 - Trevor, 2

At least 25 of the young parents interviewed for this
book had belonged to a gang. Most were no longer involved. Not one father or one mother told me s/he wanted
her/his son or daughter in a gang.

They talked about strategies which might prevent their
child from going this route. They stressed the importance of
staying involved with one's child, of "being there" for
that child.

They talked about their parents who were too busy or too
poor to support them in school or community activities, and
of the difference being involved in sports, for example,
might have made in their lives:

*We want Dakota in sports. I believe the coach will
teach the children the right way, teach them discipline, to be on time, to work hard. I noticed a difference when I was in sports and when I wasn't. When I*

was in sports, I got to meet a lot more people, and school became more interesting.

You have to keep up your grades, and when I was keeping up my grades, I was learning more. When I wasn't in sports, I stayed home and watched TV. The road didn't seem to be going anywhere. I was just there.

Nathan, 20 - Dakota, 11 months

They also talked a lot about love, and of the importance of expressing that love to their child.

I think the basic thing in raising a child is love. I think he'll get far in life if he knows he can always come home and have a good home-cooked meal with his family. And he won't need to go looking for a gang or be out on the streets because he'll be secure in himself.

I've seen a lot of parents say, "My daughter is in a gang. I give up." If they could just say to that daughter, "I love you." Three little words could change so much.

Camelia, 16 - Buchanan, 6 months

The relationship you build with your child is the most important factor in protecting him from gangs and violence. For more on this subject, see "Teaching Your Child to Be Non-Violent," chapter 10, *Discipline from Birth to Three* by Lindsay and McCullough.

Getting Out

There are a lot of gangs in this neighborhood, a lot of violence around here. The other day they killed a guy right here on my street.

My boyfriend was a gang member before, and he lost a lot of friends. His best friend died in his arms.

Almost everybody in his gang is either dead or in jail.
He changed after he met me. When he met me he
had just come out of jail. After that I got pregnant,
and he hasn't gone back to jail for four years. Before
that, every six months he was back in jail.

Mariaeliza, 17 - Vincent, 3

Some gangs make it extremely difficult for a member to get out. If you're in that situation, and you'd like to change your lifestyle, have you considered leaving your neighborhood? For some people, that appears to be the best solution. It's also likely to be an extremely difficult decision. Even if you'd like to leave, where would you go?

Is there a relative or close family friend who might take you in? Is an older sibling thinking of moving out, and might take you along? How about getting a roommate or other couple to move out of the area with you? Even a few miles away can make all the difference.

If you have no resources, and neither your parents, your relatives, your partner, or your friends can/will help you, you need to go elsewhere for help. Former chief of Police Richard Tefank, Buena Park, California, commented, "Getting out takes trying to get some help. If you want to leave the neighborhood bad enough, I think you can.

"That can mean contacting local churches. At least you'd get some support there, and if you need to talk to somebody, it's a good place to go.

"Next, I'd try Child Protective Services. You go there and say, 'I want to get out of this environment with my child. Who could help me?' You aren't going as a Protective Services client. You're going there to seek help, and you might get a supportive social worker who might think, 'I'll help this person because if I don't, they may become my client.'

"I would also suggest contacting law enforcement

because they're always aware of a lot of resources. If you don't have financial resources, no family support, it's going to be tough."

You might also find help by contacting some of the other helping resources listed in chapter 14.

Lonnie had an extensive history of arrests, incarceration, placement in a series of foster homes. Only when she became pregnant did she change her life. She moved back in with her mother, and for the first time in many years, developed a good relationship with her. Lonnie went back to school, even won an achievement award from a local philanthropic organization. She credits her teacher and her mother for helping her, but most of all, she credits a detective in her community:

> *I was supposed to get busted because I left the foster home. One of the detectives who had busted me when I was real young, I think saw through me from the very beginning. I think he saw me as something more than a wanna-be.*
>
> *When he came to my friend's house to look for me, he said, "I know there is something more, and I need to give you a chance to find that something."*
>
> *When he told me that, it kind of made sense. Then after I got pregnant, he talked to my mom. To this day, ever since he told me that, I haven't messed up. I want to give back to society. To me, he was kind of like a guardian angel. I talk to him all the time. He calls to check up on me.*
>
> Lonnie

Help *is* available, but you may have to work hard at finding the help you need to enable you to have the life you want for you and your child. *You and your child are worth the effort!*

Graduating is an important gift to yourself and your child.

14

Your Future —
Your Child's Future

- **Looking Ahead**
- **Taking Financial Responsibility**
- **Value of Education**
- **Non-Traditional Jobs**
- **After High School**
- **Job Aids Self-Esteem**
- **Who Stays Home?**
- **Heavy Expense of Moving Out**
- **Money vs. Happiness**
- **Other Problems**
- **Finding Community Resources**
- **Don't Give Up**
- **Pregnancy/Marital Counseling**
- **Writing Life Script**

I used to hate school, but now it's different having Vincent. I want to go to college because I want to be a better person for my future and for his.

I didn't have a good relationship with my parents. I felt like I was by myself in this world. Vincent has made a big difference in my life. Now I have somebody here for me.

Mariaeliza, 17 - Vincent, 3

I'll graduate this year, then get myself into college. I want to be a social worker, work with people who get food stamps. I've always liked to work with people, people with real needs.

For awhile I stopped going to school, and I'd feel like everybody was against me. Then they told me there was a teen mom program, so I went. I started school late, in November, and I'd go for a month, then for a month I'd not go. But when I had my baby, I got into school.

I always hated school, I hate waking up, I was always grouchy. But once I had my kid, I changed to the opposite because I knew everything I learned was for her. I feel at home at school now.

Clancy Jane, 17 - Jenae, 23 months

Looking Ahead

Your child may be three soon. What kind of future are you planning for him and for yourself? If you're with his other parent, are you following your dreams of a satisfying life together? Are you already an independent family, or on your way to becoming independent?

If you're by yourself or with another partner, what are your plans for your future? Are you able to support your child if you need to do so? If you aren't to that point, what are you doing now to get there? Are you still in school? Are you learning job skills? Whether you're your child's mother or father, it's essential that you be able to support yourself and your child.

Even if she's married, the girl should get a job and learn to be independent, especially the way so many are getting divorced today. If she never knew anything, dropped out of school because she got pregnant, and got married, the only thing she's learning is cleaning and cooking. Beyond that, she doesn't know much if she doesn't ever get a job.

I didn't feel good about myself at first when I knew
I was pregnant. Later, I thought of the way I was, and
I decided I didn't want Janis to grow up the way I did.

I had to change a lot of my attitudes, and think
what I wanted to do to change myself.

So often the mother is going to support the child. I
like to work because it makes me feel more indepen-
dent. I don't have to rely on anybody else.

Darla, 17 - Janis, 2

Taking Financial Responsibility

I was working a construction job, making just a
little over minimum wage. I thought, "Here we are,
bringing a child into the world, and I'm going to have
to support the child." I told the construction crew I
was going to be a dad, and I wanted some advice.

"Leave now," they told me.

And "Get an abortion."

I hung in there, and when Francene was born, we
had benefits, so the medical bills were paid. But so
much else was on my mind. Will I be able to afford
food? The bills? The responsibilities never end.

I was worried about being a father. How do you fill
a father's shoes, someone who's supposed to have all
the answers? How do you live up to a father's
reputation?

Julio, 24 - Francene, 4; Alina, 3; Gloria, 1

Some teenage fathers and mothers aren't supporting their
child because they're still in school. Others have dropped
out, but can't find a good job. The best approach for them
is to stay in or go back to school and/or get job training to
prepare themselves for supporting their family.

Julio had a low-paying job and, like many other young

fathers, wondered how he could ever support his family.

Whether you're the mother or the father, you need to live up to a parenting "reputation," as Julio says. You'll never have all the answers — none of us do — but you'll need to be responsible for your child. Being responsible includes being financially responsible.

> *I thought it was going to be all easy. I thought I was going to coast through it (parenting). I've had a lot of hard times, times when I was broke and wondered how my son was going to eat, get diapers. I usually found a job, not enough money for myself, but enough so my son would have what he needed.*
>
> *My plan before Dorian was born, before I even thought about having a baby, was to go to college and be an architect, but I got sidetracked. I'm still going to college.*
>
> *Now I'm working as a custom plasterer. The pay is pretty good, but for a life-time career, no.*
>
> Riley, 18 - Dorian, 11 months

Importance of Education

> *I went back to school because I have to graduate for my son. Barnaby's dad didn't graduate, so I'm the one that has to. How would I give my son help when he comes home and does his math? I had to go back to school.*
>
> Bridget, 18 - Barnaby, 6 months

Women who achieve at least a high school education are only half as likely to live in households receiving TANF (Temporary Aid to Needy Families) as are women who never graduated. If the young mother depends on welfare payments, there is never enough money. Now, with welfare reform, eligibility for help from welfare is severely limited.

*When I moved in with my husband, I stopped going
to school. I went back after Buchanan was born
because I started thinking. I want to get a good job. I
want to have a college education. I want to show
Buchanan that I've done good with my life. I want to
get a job so I can help support him financially as well
as emotionally.*

Camelia, 16 - Buchanan, 6 months

Sharon, too, decided to return to school:

*I'd been out of school for two years. I saw some-
thing at the store about this school for teen parents. I
wrote down the number, went home, and called. I'm
back in school now, and they take care of my kids.*

*I need an education for my kids so I can get a good
job. If my kids want to ask me something, I want to be
able to answer them. I want the best for them. My
husband wants me in school, too.*

Sharon, 19 - Ricardo, 35 months; Monique, 16 months

Sharon is lucky. She lives in a school district which
provides childcare for students' infants and toddlers.

If your school doesn't have a childcare center, and you
don't have a relative or friend who will care for your child
while you continue school, what will you do? See *Your
Baby's First Year* for tips on choosing suitable day care for
your child and suggestions on handling the expense of
that care.

Non-Traditional Jobs for Women

*I dropped out of school when I was five months
pregnant with Celeste. Then, when I got pregnant
again, my sister found out about the Teen Parent
Program and said I should go.*

I said, "I'm not going. They'll put me down for
having a second kid when I'm so young."

But they didn't, and everybody understands where
I'm coming from.

I don't want another baby for awhile. I want to
have a career. I want to be a mechanic, although my
father wants me to think of something else. Our
Community College waives fees for single parents.

Noelle-Marie, 19 - Celeste, 21/2; Carrie, 9 months

Noelle-Marie's desire to be a mechanic could be a smart
choice. Teen parents need jobs that pay family-supporting
wages. High-paying jobs for high school graduates are
usually in the technical fields, or in occupations considered
non-traditional for women.

Jobs and careers traditionally dominated by men tend to
pay higher wages and salaries than those traditionally held
by women, even when the education required for "male"
and "female" occupations is similar. Samples of non-
traditional occupations for women are the technical trades
of carpenter, plumber, auto/diesel technician, law
enforcement, and fire fighting.

If you are a young mother and your parents, like Noelle-
Marie's father, don't like the idea of you becoming a
mechanic or a plumber, research comparative pay of various kinds of work. Also figure out what it will cost you and
your child to live as you would like to live. Share the
results with your parents. A non-traditional career could be
the route to a more satisfying lifestyle for you and your
family.

Most of my friends who have had a baby have
dropped out of school. It bothers me a lot. Two of my
good friends who dropped out will be working at fast-
food places or a store, and that's not going to support

their children.

I don't know if I'll be with my baby's dad forever, and I don't want to have to depend on his income. I want to be able to live on my own.

Lyra, 18 - Leah, 2 1/2

After High School, What?

Often it's important not to put off getting your education. If you've already graduated from high school, you may decide to go ahead with further training as soon as possible.

Shirley graduated from high school three years ago when Virginia was fourteen months old. Because she had learned office skills in high school, Shirley started working for the county in the welfare department a few months later. After working directly with people applying for welfare, she has some firm opinions on the subject:

You don't get anywhere on welfare. I hear people saying, "I have these two children who are starving and. . ." All I can say is, if you care for yourself as a person, and for those children, you'll go out there and work. I could never get what I want waiting for a check on the first and the fifteenth. I couldn't live off what somebody else gives me just because I have a baby. I want a lot of things for me and my daughter.

Shirley, 20 - Virginia, 4

Remember, if you complete high school, your chances of being on welfare are half what they are if you drop out before you graduate.

Parents, fathers as well as mothers, who continue their education and hold good jobs obviously are much better off than are parents who quit school, and whose only income is their temporary TANF grant.

I stayed in school. You got to go to school so you can get the kind of job you want. I'm not on welfare — never was. When paycheck time comes around, I'm out of money, but I'm getting there. It's being independent that counts.

I want to be an administrative secretary, so I'll be going to junior college for the next two years.

Ginger, 18 - Sean, 17 months

His parents are working hard to give him a good life.

Job Helps Self-Esteem

Many young parents also discussed the difference a job can make in the way they feel about themselves. They often mentioned that when a mother thinks well of herself, when she has good self-esteem, she's a better mother than she is when she's unhappy with herself.

When Martha was little, we stayed by ourselves for almost a year. I was home most of the time, watching TV and being bored. At that time, I wasn't helping myself. I was depending on my parents plus welfare.

Now I'm self-supporting. I feel good about myself because I'm doing it on my own. I've found out I can cope, and I love my job. I'm a nurse's assistant, and I'm taking a medical terminology class.

I think I'm a better mother when I like myself.

Alta, 22 - Martha, 6; Howard, 3

Of course this applies to fathers, also. Many young men have difficulty finding a job which pays enough to support their family. Whether you're a mother or a father, the importance of workforce preparation cannot be over-emphasized.

Have you already dropped out of school? Now, this minute, is the time to return. You can go back to your regular school or to a special class for teen parents — if there is such a school in your area.

In most states, if you're 18 or older, you can go to a local community college to take classes to help you earn your high school diploma. Check community college catalogs for job training facilities. Possibilities may include Regional Occupation Programs (ROP) and high school career centers. You may find help with child care or transportation, especially if you qualify for TANF. Talk to your social worker.

Who Stays Home with the Kids?

If you're with a partner, both of you may need to work simply to be able to pay your bills. Or one of you may decide to stay home with your child(ren) while the other one keeps a job.

In traditional families, the mother stays home and takes care of the children and cleans the house. If they can afford it, many families still prefer to have a parent home while the children are young.

Either the mother or the father can care for the children, and either the mother or father can support the family. More often today, however, parents share both roles.

Heavy Expense of Moving Out

Living with your own parents is often difficult when you have a child yourself. Wanting to move into a place of one's own is certainly an understandable goal. If you've never lived on your own, if your parents have always paid the bills, you may not realize how expensive it is to keep an apartment.

> *I plan to move out in three months when Holly (friend with a baby) turns 18. I'm 15. Hopefully, I can get $350 from welfare. An apartment will be $500 a month, and I'll split that with Holly. Then we can go half on the groceries, and Robin will be eating table food by then. We should be able to make it.*
>
> Melinda, 15 - Robin, 9 months

First, it is doubtful that Melinda will be able to receive welfare if she moves out at age 15. In most states, a mother under 18 must live with her parents in order to qualify for TANF. If Melinda can get money on her own, she and Holly may still have trouble renting an apartment. Apartment owners often choose not to rent to young single mothers and their children, especially if they must rely on welfare for their income.

Second, Melinda doesn't appear to be planning realistically for her other expenses. She and Holly need to talk to other young families who live on their own. What do they actually spend for food? What about transportation? Clothing? Emergency expenses?

The high cost of living independently may be unreal to you. Or that high cost may be the biggest reason you're still with your parents.

Money versus Happiness

Money doesn't buy happiness, but the lack of "enough" money can certainly cause a great deal of unhappiness. As you plan your future, it's important that you plan how you'll earn enough money to support your child.

Even if the two parents are together and both are working, they may have heavy financial problems:

We had credit, and we got deeper and deeper in debt. When we finally wrote it down in black and white, we had $2600 debts each month, but we brought in only $1900.

We wrote letters, trying to be rational. That didn't help. They picked up all our furniture, and we filed for bankruptcy a year ago.

It was hard on the kids when the furniture went. We had no refrigerator. We slept on the floor on a mattress and ate out of an icebox. How do you explain that to kids?

After filing for bankruptcy, your credit is ruined for seven to ten years. You have to get a co-signer or have a lot of collateral in order to get credit.

We scrimp from week to week. We're just not

*money managers at all. What we're trying now is for
Denver to hold the checkbook. He keeps it so I can't
write checks.*

*The worst thing you can do is to file for bank-
ruptcy. I would sell everything in my house before I'd
do that again.*

*I would go to a credit counselor, but Denver won't
go. He thinks we should be able to manage it
ourselves — but we're not.*

*It's just that hard. The important thing is to man-
age your money. I think we should be teaching money
management in the schools.*

Mitzi, 22 - Selene, 5; Vaughn, 2

Whatever your income, you might think about Mitzi's
last comment. Sometimes a class in money management
can help a person plan how best to budget her income. If
you think you're heading for financial trouble, get help.
Don't coast along until you have the big money problems
facing Mitzi, Denver, and their children.

You may be able to find a non-profit group offering
credit counseling in your community. Be careful of credit
counselors who charge big fees.

Look under "Debt Counseling" or a similar heading in
your telephone directory. Try to find someone who, at little
or no charge, will help you work out a plan to budget
your income.

With some professional help, plus lots of effort on your
part, you may be able to pull out of seemingly hopeless
money problems.

When You Have Other Problems
Not all problems come with dollar signs. Teen parents,
like everyone else, have ups and downs in their lives.

You may already be in school, or you may have a job. You may be making plans for your future and for your child's future.

If, however, your life is not going the way you want it to go, have you considered getting extra help? You don't have to handle everything by yourself.

> *It's hard being a single parent. We were living together for awhile, and I miss the emotional support.*
>
> *When I get really uptight, I put Juanita in the crib and let her cry. There's nothing I can do unless I hold her all day, and then I'm more upset.*
>
> Esperanza, 17 - Juanita, 12 months

If you're having more problems than you can handle by yourself, the first step is to accept the fact that you need help. Some people find it very hard to admit they aren't making it on their own.

You're probably already getting informal help. Families often are a good source of support. So are friends. In fact, other young parents can offer tremendous support simply because they're facing some of the same problems that are bothering you.

Finding Community Resources

You may need help beyond what your family and friends can give. Perhaps they can suggest community resources for you to contact. Inquire about resources from other people with whom you interact — the director of a childcare center, your minister, doctor, or teacher.

Also check your telephone book. Your county or state Mental Health Association and Psychology Department at your local college may recommend counseling services.

If you're receiving TANF (welfare), ask to see a social worker when you need special help. Social workers often have far too heavy case loads, but some are able to provide extra help to their clients. If you have a local community center, the social worker there may be able to tell you where to go for help with your problems. Your hospital social service department may be a good resource.

More than 300 agencies in the United States are connected with the Family Service Association of America. These agencies offer individual and family counseling at low cost, as well as a variety of other family services.

For the agency in your area, check your telephone directory under the following listings: Family Service Association, Council for Community Services, County Department of Health, Counseling Clinic, Mental Health Clinic, or United Way.

Don't Give Up

Generally you can get a list of hot lines from your telephone operator. Call Information (411 or, for toll-free numbers, 1.800.555.1212), then say, "I have this type of problem. Can you help me?"

You may find, as you call hot lines and other community services, that phone numbers you have been given are not helping you. Too often the number has been changed, your call is answered by a recording, or the person responding tells you that agency can't help you.

When this happens, don't give up. If a person answers your call but can't help, ask for referrals. Tell him/her you need help. You don't know where to call next. Explain how much you would appreciate any ideas s/he may give you.

Pregnancy and Marital Counseling

If you're pregnant unexpectedly, your community probably has several agencies specifically organized to help you and others in your situation. Call the Planned Parenthood

Association, Florence Crittenton Services, Catholic
Charities, or family or children's services. Or talk to your
guidance counselor, your doctor, or your pastor, priest,
rabbi, imam, or other religious leader.

If you are a single parent, find out if there is a support
group for single parents in your community. Check with the
above resources for information about such groups. In
some areas, Children's Home Society sponsors single
parent support groups.

Marriage and family counselors are usually listed in the
telephone yellow pages. Your community may have a cost-
free counseling agency, or the cost may be based on your
income. If you have very little income, you may not be
charged a fee.

Independence and self-sufficiency are wonderful things
— if they work. All of us need extra help at some time. If
this is your time of special need, do whatever is necessary
to get that help. Both you and your child will be glad
you did.

Writing Your Life Script

*You get tired, but you can work, you can go to
school, you can be with your child. You just have to
work it into your schedule.*

Brynn, 17 - Brent, 17 months

Some people feel that a young woman who has a child
when she is 16 is doomed to a life of poverty and unhappiness. They point out that the young mother will probably
drop out of school and won't be able to find a steady job, a
job which pays enough to provide for herself and her child.
She may feel she has to get married. Her life choices seem
quite limited.

If a teenage parent can, however, continue her education,

improve her vocational skills, find a job, and, when she is ready, marry someone she wants to marry, her life script (life plan) can be quite different.

I feel old compared to when I was first pregnant. I look at life differently. I have two children, so I can't just go around not knowing what I want to do with my life. I'm more responsible now, and every minute counts.

I work and I go to school. I'm not influenced by my friends like I used to be. Some people, even though they have children, go on with their lives as if their parents are going to take care of the child.

It doesn't work that way with me. On both sides our parents don't take the responsibility of raising our kids. I think it's good they don't. If they did, I would be taking it for granted and leaving them with my parents all the time.

Mary, 21 - Shawna, 4; Ahmud, 20 months

Most of the young parents in this book are not settling for a life of hardship because of early childbearing. Instead, many are continuing their education and are acquiring job skills. They are not accepting a life script filled with poverty and unhappiness. They *are* finding that "writing" — and living — a successful life script is a difficult task.

Even very young parents can be in charge of their life scripts . . . if they continue their education and acquire vocational skills. For most young parents, this will be very difficult, but well worth the effort.

You and your child deserve the best there is. If you get your education and improve your vocational skills, you can be in charge of your life script.

More power to you!

Appendix

About the Author

Jeanne Warren Lindsay is the author of sixteen books for and about pregnant and parenting teens. Almost 700,000 copies of her books have been sold.

Lindsay's books deal with teenage pregnancy, parenting, adoption from the birthfamily's perspective, and teen relationships. Her *Teen Dads: Rights, Responsibilities and Joys* was selected by the American Library Association as a Recommended Book for Reluctant Young Adult Readers.

Lindsay has worked with hundreds of pregnant and parenting teenagers. She developed the Teen Parent Program at Tracy High School, Cerritos, California, and coordinated the program for many years. Most of her books are written for pregnant and parenting teens, and quotes from interviewees are frequently used to illustrate concepts.

Lindsay grew up on a farm in Kansas. She has lived in the same house in Buena Park, California, for 43 years. She loves to visit the Middle West, but says she's now addicted to life in southern California. She and her husband, Bob, have five children and seven grandchildren.

Lindsay is the editor of *PPT Express*, a quarterly newsletter for teachers and others working with pregnant and parenting teens. She speaks frequently at conferences across the country, but says she is happiest while interviewing young people for her books or writing under the big elm tree in her backyard.

Bibliography

The following bibliography contains books of interest to pregnant and parenting teens. Workbooks and other classroom aids are available for some of these titles.

Prices in late 2003 are quoted. Because prices change so rapidly, however, and because publishers move, call your local book store, check with an internet book store, or call your library reference department for an updated price. If you can't find a book in your bookstore, you can usually get it directly from the publisher. Enclose $3 for shipping per book. See page 223 for an order form for Morning Glory Press publications.

Anasar, Eleanor. **"You and Your Baby: Playing and Learning Together." "You and Your Baby: A Special Relationship."** 2001. **"You and Your Baby: The Toddler Years."** 2003. 32 pp. each. Each available in Spanish edition. $2.65 each. Bulk discounts. The Corner Health Center, 47 North Huron Street, Ypsilanti, MI 48197. 734.484.3600.
Gorgeous photos of teen parents and their children on every other page. Each booklet contains helpful information at an extremely easy reading level.

Arnoldi, Katherine. *The Amazing True Story of a Teenage Single Mom.* 1998. 176 pp. $16. Hyperion.
Written in a true experience/comic book format, it's the story of a young mom who had dreams, but faced many obstacles in fulfilling them.

Beaglehole, Ruth. *Mama, listen! Raising a Child without Violence: A Handbook for Teen Parents.* 1998. 224 pp. $25. Curriculum Guide, $20. Ruth Beaglehole, 2162 Echo Park Ave., Los Angeles, CA 90026. 323.661.9123.
A unique book. Most of it is written as if a toddler is speaking, explaining what s/he needs from his/her parents. Good description of emotional needs of small children. An absolute lack of violence (no spanking) is recommended throughout.

Harris, Robie H. Illus. by Michael Emberley. *It's Perfectly Normal: Changing Bodies, Growing Up, Sex and Sexual Health.* 1996. 89 pp. $10.99. Candlewick Press.
The illustrations are wonderful, and make it difficult to continue thinking of sex as something we never talk about with our children.

Heart to Heart Program. For information, contact Heart to Heart, Ounce of Prevention Fund, 122 South Michigan Avenue, Ste. 2050, Chicago, IL 60603. 312/922-3863.
An innovative approach to preventing child sexual abuse by teaching teen parents to protect their children from abuse. Program can be implemented in a school or community-based setting. Practitioners participate in a two-day training and purchase the curriculum and facilitator's guide.

Jacobs, Thomas A., et al. *What Are My Rights? 95 Questions and Answers about Teens and the Law.* 1997. 208 pp. $14.95. Free Spirit Publishing. 612.338.2068.
A matter-of-fact guide to the laws that affect teens at home, at school, on the job, and in their communities.

Lansky, Vicki. *Getting Your Child to Sleep . . . and Back to Sleep.* 1991. 132 pp. $6.95. The Book Peddlers, 15245 Minnetonka Boulevard, Deep Haven, MN 55345-1510. 1-800/255-3379.
Book offers a wealth of suggestions for dealing with babies and small children who don't sleep as regularly as their parents would like.

Leach, Penelope. *Your Baby and Child from Birth to Age Five.* Revised, 1997. 560 pp. $20. Alfred A. Knopf.
An absolutely beautiful book packed with information, many color photos

and lovely drawings. Comprehensive, authoritative, and outstandingly sensitive guide to child care and development.

Lieberman, E. James, M.D., and Karen Lieberman Troccoli, M.P.H. *Like It Is: A Teen Sex Guide.* 1998. 216 pp. $25. McFarland and Co. *Excellent book to offer teen parents (all teens actually). It describes methods of contraception, starting with abstinence, and the risks associated with each one. Gives bias-free information about pregnancy options.*

Lindsay, Jeanne Warren. *The Challenge of Toddlers* and *Your Baby's First Year (Teens Parenting* **Series).** 2004. 224 pp. each. Paper, $12.95 each; hardcover, $18.95 each. Workbooks, $2.50 each. Quantity discounts. Morning Glory Press. 888.612.8254. *How-to-parent books especially for teenage parents. Lots of quotes from teenage parents who share their experiences. Board games ($29.95 each), one for each of these titles, provide great learning reinforcement. Also see four-video series, Your Baby's First Year. For detailed teaching guides, see* **Challenge of Toddlers** *and* **Nurturing Your Newborn/Your Baby's First Year Comprehensive Curriculum Notebooks.**

_____. *Do I Have a Daddy? A Story About a Single-Parent Child.* 2000. 48 pp. Paper, $7.95; hardcover, $14.95. Free study guide. Morning Glory Press. *A beautiful full-color picture book for the child who has never met his/her father. A special sixteen-page section offers suggestions to single mothers.*

_____. *Teen Dads: Rights, Responsibilities and Joys (Teens Parenting* **Series).** 2001. 224 pp. $12.95. Workbook, $2.50. Quantity discounts. Morning Glory Press. *A how-to-parent book especially for teenage fathers. Offers help in parenting from conception to age 3 of the child. Many quotes from and photos of teen fathers. For detailed teaching help, see* **Teen Dads Comprehensive Curriculum Notebook.**

_____. *Teenage Couples — Caring, Commitment and Change: How to Build a Relationship that Lasts. Teenage Couples — Coping with Reality: Dealing with Money, In-laws, Babies and Other Details of Daily Life.* 1995. 208, 192 pp. Paper, $9.95 ea.; hardcover, $15.95 ea. Workbooks, $2.50 ea. Curriculum Guide, $19.95. Morning Glory Press. *Series covers such important topics as communication, handling arguments, keeping romance alive, sex in a relationship, jealousy, alcohol and drug addiction, partner abuse, and divorce, as well as the practical details of living. Lots of quotes from teenage couples.*

_____ and Jean Brunelli. *Nurturing Your Newborn: Young Parent's*

Guide to Baby's First Month. (Teens Parenting **Series***)* 1999. 96
pp. $6.95. Workbook, $2. Quantity discounts. Morning Glory Press.
*Focuses on the postpartum period. Ideal for teen parents home after
delivery. For detailed teaching help, see* **Nurturing Your Newborn/Your
Baby's First Year Comprehensive Curriculum Notebook***.*

_____, _____ . **Your Pregnancy and Newborn Journey (Teens
Parenting** **Series).** 2004. 224 pp. Paper, $12.95; hardcover, $18.95;
Workbook, $2.50. Quantity discounts. Morning Glory Press.
*Prenatal health book for pregnant teens. Includes section on care of new-
born and chapter for fathers. For detailed teaching help, see* **Your
Pregnancy and Newborn Journey Comprehensive Curriculum Notebook***.*
Also see **Pregnancy and Newborn Journey board game** and **Pregnancy
Two-in-One Bingo game**.

_____ and Sally McCullough. **Discipline from Birth to Three.** 2004.
224 pp. Paper, $12.95; hardcover, $18.95. Workbook, $2.50. Morning
Glory Press.
*Provides teenage parents with guidelines to help prevent discipline problems
with children and for dealing with problems when they occur. For detailed
teaching help, see* **Discipline from Birth to Three Comprehensive Curriculum Notebook***.* Also see 4-video series, **Discipline from Birth to Three.**

Marecek, Mary. **Breaking Free from Partner Abuse.** 1999. 96 pp.
$8.95. Quantity discount. Morning Glory Press.
*Lovely edition illustrated by Jami Moffett. Underlying message is that the
reader does not deserve to be hit. Simply written. Can help a young woman
escape an abusive relationship.*

MELD Parenting Materials. **Nueva Familia.** Six books, each in
Spanish and English editions. **Baby Is Here. Feeding Your Child, 5
months-2 years. Healthy Child, Sick Child. Safe Child and Emer-
gencies. Baby Grows. Baby Plays.** 1992. $12 each. MELD, Suite
507, 123 North Third St., Minneapolis, MN 55401. 612.332.7563.
*Very easy to read books full of information. Designed especially for
Mexican and Mexican American families, but excellent for anyone with
limited reading skills. Ask MELD for catalog of other materials designed
especially for school-age parents.*

_____. **The New Middle of the Night Book: Answers to Young
Parents' Questions When No One Is Around.** 1999. 163 pp. $12.50.
MELD.
*Includes clearly written information about parenting during the first two
years of life. An especially good section discusses the benefits and how-tos
of shared parenting, whether or not the parents are together as a couple.*

_____. *The Safe, Self-Confident Child.* 1997. $8.95. MELD.
Important information on how to protect children from harm, and ways to help children improve their self-confidence.

Parent Express Series: *Parent Express: For You and Your Infant. Spanish edition: Noticlas para los padres. Parent Express: For You and Your Toddler.* Each newsletter, 8 pp. $4 each set. ANR Publications, University of California, 6701 San Pablo Avenue, Oakland, CA 94608-1239. 510.642.2431.
Wonderful series of newsletters for parents. The first set starts two months before delivery, and continues monthly through the first year of the child's life. Second set with twelve letters covers second and third years. Good resource for teen parents. Beautiful photos, easy reading.

Pollock, Sudie. *Will the Dollars Stretch? Teen Parents Living on Their Own.* 2001. 112 pp. $7.95. Teacher's Guide, $2.50. Morning Glory.
Five short stories about teen parents moving out on their own. As students read, they will get the feel of poverty as experienced by many teen parents — as they write checks and balance checkbooks of young parents involved.

_____. *Moving On: Finding Information You Need for Living on Your Own.* 2001. 48 pp. $4.95. 25/$75. Morning Glory Press.
Fill-in guide to help young persons find information about their community, information needed for living away from parents.

Porter, Connie. *Imani All Mine.* 1999. 218 pp. $12. Houghton Miflin.
Wonderful novel about a black teen mom in the ghetto where poverty, racism, and danger are constant realities.

Reynolds, Marilyn. **True-to-Life Series from Hamilton High.** *Baby Help. Beyond Dreams. But What About Me? Detour for Emmy. Telling. Too Soon for Jeff, Love Rules, If You Loved Me.* 1993-2001. 160-256 pp. Paper, $8.95 each (*Love Rules,* $9.95). Morning Glory Press.
Wonderfully gripping stories about situations faced by teens. Start with **Detour for Emmy,** *award-winning novel about a 15-year-old mother. Students who read one of Reynolds' novels usually ask for more. Topics cover partner abuse, acquaintance rape, reluctant teen father, sexual molestation, racism, fatal accident, abstinence, homophobia, school failure.*

Rodriguez, Luis J. *Always Running — La vida loca: Gang Days in L. A.* 1993. 260 pp. $11. Touchstone, Rockefeller Center, 1230 Avenue of the Americas, New York, NY 10020.
The author tells his own story of gang life in East L.A. in the 70s. It's a vivid memoir that explores the motivations of gang life and cautions

against the death and destruction that inevitably claim its participants. Helps reader understand the reasons young people join gangs, and the difficulties of breaking free.

Seward, Angela. Illustrated by Donna Ferreiro. ***Goodnight, Daddy.*** 2001. 48 pp. Paper, $7.95; hardcover, $14.95. Morning Glory Press. *Beautiful full-color picture book shows Phoebe's excitement because of her father's visit today. She is devastated when he calls to say "Something has come up." Book illustrates the importance of father in the life of his child.*

Silberg, Jackie. ***125 Brain Games for Babies.*** 1999. 143 pp. $14.95. Consortium Book Sales. ***125 Brain Games for Toddlers and Twos.*** 2000. $14.95. Gryphon House. *Packed with everyday games, songs, and other opportunities to encourage the brain development of children from birth through three years. Illustrated.*

Spock, Benjamin, M.D., and Steven J. Parker, M.D. ***Dr. Spock's Baby and Child Care.*** 1998. 939 pp. $7. Pocket Books, a division of Simon & Schuster Inc. *Generations of parents have relied on Dr. Spock's bestseller as their parenting sourcebook. Now updated and expanded.*

Stewart, Nancy. ***Your Baby from Birth to 18 Months: The Complete Illustrated Guide.*** 1997. 192 pp. $17. Perseus Publishing. *Provides clear and valid information about caring for the new baby up to age 18 months. Well illustrated.*

Williams, Kelly. ***Single Mamahood: Advice and Wisdom for the African American Single Mother.*** 1998. 190 pp. $12. Carol Publishing Group, 120 Enterprise Avenue, Secaucus, NJ 07094. *Down-to-earth, sister-to-sister guide. Offers suggestions on how to deal with work, school, child support, discipline, dating again, and more.*

Wolff, Virginia E. ***Make Lemonade.*** 1995. 208 pp. $15.95. Holt. *Wonderful novel about teenager living in a Project who takes a job baby-sitting for a teenage mom, and who eventually sees the mom back in school, her children in child care, and her life back on focus.*

Index

Morning Glory Press
6595 San Haroldo Way, Buena Park, CA 90620
714.828.1998; 888.612.8254   Fax 714.828.2049
Contact us for complete catalog including quantity and other discounts.

		Price	Total
__ *Complete* **Teens Parenting Curriculum**		$1085.00	_____

One each — Five *Comprehensive Curriculum Notebooks*
plus 8 books, 6 workbooks, 8 videos, 4 games
(everything on this order form except last 13 titles as noted on p. 2)
Buy a text and workbook for each student.
Contact us for generous quantity discounts.

Resources for Teen Parent Teachers/Counselors:

__ *Books, Babies and School-Age Parents*				
		1-885356-22-6	14.95	_____
__ *ROAD to Fatherhood*		1-885356-92-7	14.95	_____

Resources for Teen Parents:

Your Pregnancy and Newborn Journey				
__	Paper	1-932538-00-3	12.95	
__	Hardcover	1-932538-01-1	18.95	_____
__	Workbook	1-932538-02-x	2.50	_____
__ *PNJ Curriculum Notebook*		1-885356-96-x	125.00	_____
__ **PNJ Board Game**		1-885356-19-6	29.95	_____
__ **Pregnancy Two-in-One Bingo**		1-885356-64-1	19.95	_____
__ *Nurturing Your Newborn*		1-885356-58-7	6.95	_____
__	Workbook	1-885356-61-7	2.00	_____
Your Baby's First Year				
__	Paper	1-932538-03-8	12.95	_____
__	Hardcover	1-932538-04-6	18.95	_____
__	Workbook	1-932538-05-4	2.50	_____
__ *BFY/NN Curriculum Notebook*		1-885356-97-8	125.00	_____
Four-video series — Your Baby's First Year				
__	**Nurturing Your Newborn**	1-885356-86-2	69.95	_____
__	**She's Much More Active**	1-885356-87-0	69.95	_____
__	**Leaving Baby Stage Behind**	1-885356-88-9	69.95	_____
__	**Keeping Your Baby Healthy**	1-885356-89-7	69.95	_____
__ **All Four Videos — Baby's First Year Series**			195.00	_____
__ **Baby's First Year Board Game**		1-885356-20-x	29.95	_____
Four-video series — Discipline from Birth to Three				
__	**Infants and Discipline**	1-885356-82-x	69.95	_____
__	**He's Crawling — Help!**	1-885356-83-8	69.95	_____
__	**She's into Everything!**	1-885356-84-6	69.95	_____
__	**Your Busy Runabout**	1-885356-85-4	69.95	_____
__ **All Four Videos — Discipline Birth to Three Series**			195.00	_____

SUB-TOTAL (Carry over to top of next page) _____

SUB-TOTAL FROM PREVIOUS PAGE _____

More Resources for Teen Parents:

Discipline from Birth to Three

__	Paper	1-932538-09-7	12.95	_____
__	Hardcover	1-932538-10-0	18.95	_____
__	Workbook	1-932538-11-9	2.50	_____
__ *Discipline Curriculum Notebook*		1-885356-99-4	125.00	_____

The Challenge of Toddlers

__	Paper	1-932538-06-2	12.95	_____
__	Hardcover	1-932538-07-0	18.95	_____
__	Workbook	1-932538-08-9	2.50	_____
__ **CT Curriculum Notebook**		1-885356-98-6	125.00	_____
__ **Challenge of Toddlers Bd. Game**		1-885356-56-0	29.95	_____

Teen Dads: Rights, Responsibilities and Joys

__	Paper	1-885356-68-4	12.95	_____
__	Workbook	1-885356-69-2	2.50	_____
__ *Teen Dads Curriculum Notebook*		1-995357-95-1	125.00	_____

Following books are NOT included in Complete *Teens Parenting* Curriculum:

__ *Do I Have a Daddy?* Paper	0-885356-63-3	7.95	_____
__ *Pregnant? Adoption Is an Option*	1-885356-08-0	11.95	_____
__ *Surviving Teen Pregnancy*	1-885356-06-4	11.95	_____
__ *Teenage Couples: Caring, Commitment and Change*			
__	0-930934-93-8	9.95	_____
— *Teenage Couples: Coping with Reality*	0-930934-86-5	9.95	_____

Novels by Marilyn Reynolds:

__ *Love Rules*	1-885356-76-5	9.95	_____
__ *If You Loved Me*	1-885356-55-2	8.95	_____
__ *Baby Help*	1-885356-27-7	8.95	_____
__ *But What About Me?*	1-885356-10-2	8.95	_____
__ *Too Soon for Jeff*	0-930934-91-1	8.95	_____
__ *Detour for Emmy*	0-930934-76-8	8.95	_____
__ *Telling*	1-885356-03-x	8.95	_____
__ *Beyond Dreams*	1-885356-00-5	8.95	_____

TOTAL _____

Add postage: 10% of total—Min., $3.50; 15%, Canada _____
California residents add 7.75% sales tax _____

TOTAL _____

Ask about quantity discounts, teacher, student guides.
Prepayment requested. School/library purchase orders accepted.
If not satisfied, return in 15 days for refund.

NAME _____

PHONE_____ Purchase Order #_____

ADDRESS _____

_____